ALONG C...

COWGIRL

DARING AND ICONIC WOMEN
OF THE RODEO & WILD WEST SHOWS

by Chris Enss

FARCOUNTRY
PRESS

ISBN: 978-1-56037-813-6

Design by Steph Lehmann

For more information about our books, write Farcountry Press, P.O. Box 5630,
Helena, MT 59604; call (800) 821-3874; or visit www.farcountrypress.com.

Library of Congress Cataloging-In-Publication data on file.

 Produced and printed in the United States of America.

26   25   24   23   22   1   2   3   4   5

CONTENTS

ACKNOWLEDGMENTS

Right out of the chute, I needed help from librarians, archivists, and photo historians to chase after information about rodeos and images from Wild West shows of long ago. I owe the following a debt of gratitude:

- Kellen Cutsforth and Tom Williamson in the Western History and Genealogy Department at the Denver Public Library.

- Bethany Dodson, Research and Education Manager at the National Cowgirl Museum and Hall of Fame.

- Wendy Polhemus-Annibell, M.S., Head Research Librarian at the Suffolk County Historical Society Library Archives in New York.

- Mack Frost at the McCracken Research Library.

- Ken Amorosano, Editor and Publisher of *Cowgirl Magazine*.

- Lauren Goss, Special Collections Public Services Librarian at the University of Oregon.

- Rachel E. Mosman, Photo Archivist and Digital Assets Manager at the Oklahoma Historical Society.

- Suzi Taylor, Reference Archivist at the Wyoming State Archives.

- Jeff Galpin, Graphic Artist at House of Print and Copy in Grass Valley, California.

- and Linda Clark, granddaughter of iconic cowgirl Hazel Hickey Moore. Thank you for sharing Hazel's story with me. ❦

FOREWORD

The iconic horsewomen of the American West, as depicted in the pages of *Along Came a Cowgirl: Daring and Iconic Women of the Rodeo & Wild West Shows*, were trailblazers in every sense of the word. Proving themselves fearless, athletic, and above all, "good horsemen," was not only a goal, but a mission in many of their lives.

Along this rough and storied path is a rare narrative that includes world records set, true stardom, and a stream of broken dreams and, in many cases, broken bones.

Adventure, freedom, and a tough American grit pursuaded many horsewomen of the early 20th century to enter the man's world of rodeo, and along with it came fame, fortune, and a hardscrabble lifestyle only the toughest could endure.

Chris Enss is a prolific chronicler of these women, giving insight to a rough-and-tumble brand of cowgirl with moxie and a lot to prove. Her mastery of getting to the core of the story is what makes Chris the gifted writer that she is.

Along Came a Cowgirl is an important historical account of the individual lives and stories that cemented the reputation and lore of the early American cowgirl, chronicled by a writer who not only knows her subject intimately but is also a trailblazer as a woman of the West. Chris Enss is well known for her historical compositions, books, and articles about women of the West and the history and times in which they lived.

With names like Mabel Strickland and Florence LaDue, these ladies were the superstars of their time, executing death-defying stunts atop speeding horses and going head-to-head with the men in bronc riding and steer wrestling competitions, much to the delight of the crowds and to the chagrin of the rodeo men.

Though competing for prize money in rodeos such as the Pendleton Round-Up and Cheyenne Frontier Days, the lure of the Wild West shows brought greater excitement and international fame.

Although they were competitors earning a living from prize money, they were entertainers more than anything, and they reveled in the accolades of screaming audiences and relished precious moments in front of royalty in places they would never have dreamed of being.

Many of the cowgirls in *Along Came a Cowgirl* attained great fame, becoming superstars in Buffalo Bill Cody's Wild West show and many others, including the 101 Ranch Wild West show, Pawnee Bill's Wild West, and Colonel Cummins' Wild West Indian Congress and Rough Riders of the World.

Not only did the young American cowgirls wow the crowds in Paris and New York, they also broke molds of the norm and set fashion trends, dressed to the nines in fancy boots, hats, scarves, colorful riding dresses, pants, and chaps. These were the true sweethearts of the rodeo, and no man would stand in their way.

Although sometimes shunned by a prudish audience of big-city ladies as unladylike for riding in pants, these spitfire mavericks were the Madonnas of their time, and they lived and reveled in every minute of it.

Along Came a Cowgirl: Daring and Iconic Women of the Rodeo & Wild West Shows is the story of these pioneering cowgirls who lived life to its fullest and whose legacy continues today in the lives of the modern-day cowgirl.

—Ken Amorosano, editor and publisher, *Cowgirl Magazine* ❦

INTRODUCTION

"Coming Soon!" read the billboards, "World Championship Rodeo! $10,000 in cash prizes! Biggest, wildest, most thrilling rodeo ever held!"

"What's a rodeo?" inquired the lady in the large, wide-brimmed hat decorated with plumes and flowers.

"Darned if I know," replied the woman in the puffed blouse and fluted skirt. "Let's go and find out."

Within the first five minutes, they got more thrills than they had ever had in all their lives before. They saw a cowboy leap from the hurricane deck* of a running horse onto the back of a galloping steer, a great, wild brute fresh from the Great Plains, weighing 900 pounds and every pound full of fight. The steers seemed to be the meanest, most devilish animals that ever walked on four feet, but they were nothing compared to the outlaw horses the women watched trying to throw riders.

This attraction called a "rodeo" was no place for a weakling. It seemed, indeed, to be a man's game, a red-blooded, two-fisted sort of a game where you would never expect to find a woman. However, the ladies were there, riding with the best of them. Outlaw horses or wild steers couldn't scare those females from the cattle country. In the beginning, rodeo events were confined to men, but it wasn't long after the exhibitions began to grow in popularity that women joined the festivities. All they needed to do to compete was prove themselves as fearless as the men, and they did.

The origins of the rodeo can be traced to the early days of the American cattle industry. Once or twice each year, cowboys rounded up cattle on the ranges and drove the herds to various marketing centers. There, in celebration of the roundups, they staged informal competitions designed to exhibit the skills of their trade. The first formal rodeo contest was held in Cheyenne in 1872; the first competition offering cash prizes was staged in Pecos, Texas, on July 4, 1883; and the first such event charging admission took place in Prescott, Arizona Territory, on July 4, 1888.

The four events contested at most of the early rodeos were saddle bronco riding, bareback bronco riding, steer wrestling, and calf roping. Other

---

*The saddle of a bucking horse

events featured included exhibitions of trick riding, shooting, and simple lassoing, as well as a number of humorous contests such as attempts to milk a wild cow or to saddle a bucking bronco.

Women began competing in rodeos as early as 1890. Many women west of the Mississippi had been roping cattle and riding broncos, along with their male counterparts, since settling in the wild frontier. It was their skill in the saddle that enabled them to find places in rodeos and perform in Wild West shows.

Wild West shows were touring the country eight years before public rodeos came into being. One of the first such shows, and certainly the most well-known, was Buffalo Bill Cody's Wild West. Organized in 1883 by William F. Cody, Buffalo Bill's show was a leading source of entertainment and education for more than thirty years. During that time of worldwide travel and countless presentations, a variety of performers captured the hearts and imaginations of fans everywhere. Among those popular entertainers were courageous women bronc riders, calf ropers, trick riders, and trick shooters.

The popularity of Buffalo Bill Cody's Wild West show prompted other businessmen to produce their own programs. Among some of the other Western-themed exhibitions were the 101 Ranch Wild West show, Pawnee Bill's Wild West, Colonel Cummins' Wild West Indian Congress and Rough Riders of the World, and Diamond Dick's Congress of World's Western

The popular 101 Ranch Wild West show, founded in 1905, was an expansion of the yearly rodeos that featured roping, riding, bulldogging, Indian dancers, trick roping, and shooting. CZARIAN CONLAN COLLECTION, COURTESY OF THE OKLAHOMA HISTORICAL SOCIETY.

Champions. Cowgirls seeking to earn their living riding wild horses, twirling lassos, and wrestling steers signed on with the various Wild West shows. Many of those cowgirls were given titles that reflected the acts in which they excelled. Posters and flyers referring to the shows' stars as "Champion Lady Bronc Rider," "Best Relay Race Rider," or "All-Around Champion Cowgirl of the World," were displayed in stores, railroad depots, restaurants, and other such establishments from coast to coast. Those labels attracted patrons, but, more often than not, the titles given to the cowgirls were unofficial.

Iconic cowgirls Fox Hastings, Tillie Baldwin, and Mabel Strickland were all billed at the same time as

PAWNEE BILL'S HISTORIC **WILD WEST SHOW**

THE AMUSEMENT TRIUMPH OF THE AGE!

SURPASSING IN TRUTHFULNESS, INTENSITY AND INSTRUCTIVE FEATURES ANY EXHIBITION OF THIS OR ANY OTHER CENTURY ON ANY CONTINENT IN THE UNIVERSE. A REALISTIC REPRODUCTION OF ACTUAL FRONTIER LIFE BY INDIANS, COWBOYS, GUIDES, OUTLAWS, TRICK ROPERS, BEAUTIFUL DARING COWGIRLS AND A DETACHMENT OF GENERAL CUSTER'S 7TH CAVALRY. THE ONLY REAL WILD WEST SHOW IN EXISTENCE. AMERICA'S NATIONAL ENTERTAINMENT. HOSTED AT PAWNEE BILL STATE PARK, MEMORIAL WEEKEND MAY 27. BEGINNING WITH A PARADE AT NOON IN DOWNTOWN PAWNEE. LIVING HISTORY EXHIBITS ALL DAY SATURDAY AND SUNDAY. SHOWTIME 5 P.M. SATURDAY.

FOR MORE INFORMATION CALL: (918) 762-2513

Pawnee Bill's Wild West show premiered in Philadelphia in the spring of 1888. AUTHOR'S COLLECTION.

HE 101 RANCH REAL WILD WEST SHOW.

est Diversified Farm and Ranch in the United States.

"Champion Lady Bulldogger." Mildred Douglas, Goldie St. Clair, and Prairie Rose Henderson were likewise labeled "Lady Bronc Riding Champion." Florence LaDue, Hazel Hickey Moore, and Bonnie Gray were all celebrated in the same time period as "Best Trick Roper." All the women were exceptional at their given talent, and all were proclaimed as top in their fields by the directors of the Wild West shows in which they rode. It wasn't until women participated in rodeo events and won that they could officially be recognized as "champion" or "best of" in whatever category they were competing in.

Lucille Mulhall was one of the first women superstars of the rodeo and Wild West shows. By the time she was eighteen, she had won numerous bronc riding and steer roping honors. In 1904, she won a gold medal for steer roping at the Cattle Convention Rodeo in Fort Worth. The three steers she roped in the show were picked out of an immense herd of wild and unruly beasts. She roped and tied the first one at one minute forty-five seconds. She cut that time down to one minute and eleven seconds with her second steer, and she dropped her third one in the remarkable time of forty seconds. Her total time for the three was three minutes and thirty-six seconds, several seconds faster than the nearest cowboy she was competing against. After her win in Texas, she was hailed as the "Queen of the Range."

Mulhall set the stage for other daring cowgirls to follow. There was Blanche McGaughey, a bronc buster for the 101 Ranch Wild West show who consistently won top honors at the Pendleton and Cheyenne rodeos and was recognized as the champion woman bronc buster of the Northwest in 1912 and 1913; Pearl Biron, a trick roper who could flick the ashes off the cigarette of a fellow performer or a flag off the head of her horse; relay racing sensation Donna Card who won multiple trophies at rodeos across the country, including the Yankee Stadium Rodeo in New York; and Lulu Parr, "Champion Lady Bucking Horse Rider of the World," who not only excelled at riding outlaw horses, but buffalo, too.

Along Came a Cowgirl: Daring and Iconic Women of the Rodeo & Wild West Shows is the story of these riding marvels from yesteryear whose names were recognized in rodeo arenas in cities and towns across the nation. Young women admired these cowgirls—women who dared to break society's traditional roles, jump aboard a horse, and hold their own in a male profession. The women included in the chapters of this volume came from a variety of backgrounds and locations, but all had in common the desire to entertain crowds on the back of their horses. With a lot of grit and determination, they were able to saddle up and follow their dreams. ◆

The Sells Floto Circus was a combination of the Floto Dog & Pony Show and the Sells Brothers Circus that toured with sideshow acts in the United States during the early 1900s. AUTHOR'S COLLECTION

PART 1

STEER ROPING

Blanche McGaughey

Bronc rider and bulldogger Blanche McGaughey sat in the chute atop a fierce quarter horse named Scar Leg. "Wait a minute," she told the cowboys sitting on either side of the gate. She smiled at the men as she tucked an embroidered handkerchief into her belt. "I don't want to lose my power puff," she told them.

"Does your nose need some nose paint?" one of the men remarked as he handed her the halter rope. The mount was released into the arena before she could respond. All eyes were on the cowgirl. Scar Leg did his best, bucking and kicking furiously, but Blanche rode like an Amazon.

Blanche's talent for riding and roping cattle was perfected at an early age while on her father's Wyoming ranch. "When I was only eight years old, I thought nothing of riding an Indian pony that had never been saddled or bridled," she told a newspaper reporter at the *Allentown Leader* in Pennsylvania in July 1914. "The cowpunchers that worked the spread always let me in on the fun when there were cattle to be rounded up. There's no place I'd rather be than the back of a horse."

Blanche's love of riding led to a job with the 101 Ranch Wild West show. In addition to bronc busting and trick roping, she also wrestled long-horned Texas steers. Her fellow performers credited her with nightly creating the "biggest thrill delivered to the audience." Blanche was devoid of nerves, strongly built, and never failed to get a "fall" out of the animal. Rodeo goers were in awe of her ability.

"The trick looks easy," Blanche explained to the *Allentown Leader* reporter, "but I can assure you it is no child's play to bring a steer to its knees and then make it turn over. Sometimes the steer will yield after a little vigorous effort, but often it requires not only the utmost brute strength, but also an infinite amount of patience and diplomacy to bring the animal down."

Blanche consistently won top honors at the Pendleton and Cheyenne rodeos and was recognized as the champion woman bronc buster of the Northwest in 1912 and 1913.

The cowgirl suffered through a number of injuries on the road to the title. She fractured her leg while relay racing at a show in Oregon and broke

Blanche McGaughey struggles to wrestle a stubborn bull to the rodeo arena floor. PH244-0068, COURTESY OF THE UNIVERSITY OF OREGON.

her wrist at a bulldogging contest in Wyoming. During a daring performance at a rodeo in Winnipeg, Snake, the bronc Blanche was riding, threw himself to the ground and rolled over on her, crushing her foot.

Blanche had a reputation for being just as tough outside the rodeo arena as she was inside it. She traveled with several well-known women riders, including Prairie Rose Henderson, Ruth Roach, and Vera McGinnis. In early 1913, Blanche got annoyed with Vera on one of their road trips and let her know how she felt about the cowgirl. The verbal altercation escalated with Blanche referring to Vera as a "chippy." The pair settled their differences with a fistfight near the horse stalls at Madison Square Garden.

Blanche retired from the rodeo profession in 1917, shortly after being named as a co-respondent in a divorce suit filed in Uniontown, Pennsylvania. ✤

Lucille Mulhall

Lucille Mulhall was fifteen years old when Vice President Theodore Roosevelt met with the Rough Riders, a regiment of men who fought with him during the Spanish-American War, for a reunion in Oklahoma City in July 1900. Her father, Colonel Zack Mulhall, owner of the expansive Mulhall Ranch and a traveling Wild West program, had arranged for the Rough Riders to see an exhibition of roping and riding by cast members from his Mulhall Wild West Show. Among the performers was his teenage daughter. Lucille had been a favorite in the cowboy exhibition for two years. Her riding talent and skill with a lariat were the envy of all the women and a fair number of men who had seen her work at fairgrounds and amphitheaters where the Mulhall Wild West Show had played. Newspapers noted she was a "remarkable girl for her age" with "wonderfully developed muscles and hands as hard as those of any cowpuncher."[1]

More than twenty-five thousand people filled the stands where the Wild West show was held. After a brief introduction, Lucille rode her sorrel horse, Governor, into the center of the arena. She then led Governor through a series of tricks she had taught him, which included picking up the wooden handle of a dinner bell with his teeth and shaking his head to ring it, rearing on his hind legs and walking, falling to the ground and "playing dead," and bowing to the audience. At the conclusion of Governor's act, Lucille retrieved the lariat hanging from his saddle and began spinning the rope. She twirled the lariat with ease, expanding the loop created with each rotation. When it was just the right size, she jumped in and out of the loop. Without missing a step, she twirled the lariat into a wider loop and swirled it out over the heads of the first few rows in the grandstand. Jerking the rope back to her, she shrunk the size of the loop while continuing to twirl it. Dropping it to her leg, she kicked the loop high, and it fell neatly over Governor's neck.[2]

The crowd went wild, cheering and applauding. Vice President Roosevelt jumped to his feet, whistling and clapping. Lucille smiled, waved at the audience, and then leapt onto Governor's back; the horse took another bow. The pair raced from the arena as the crowd continued applauding. The vice president introduced himself to her after the performance and complimented

Lucille Mulhall is recognized as America's first cowgirl. PH004_B340, COURTESY OF THE UNIVERSITY OF OREGON.

her on her talent. "Not a Rough Rider here could have done better," the politician told her.[3]

The young woman, recognized by historians as America's first cowgirl, was born on October 21, 1885, in St. Louis, Missouri. Neither she nor her parents could say for certain when she began to ride, but all could agree she lived more or less on horseback "ever since she was a little baby." Her mother Agnes was always quick to point out that, growing up, there wasn't a horse of any kind Lucille wouldn't attempt to ride. She had immense patience working with animals, and, if she did encounter a horse that seemed too difficult at first, she could tame the mount quickly with a quirt and a lasso.[4]

In addition to possessing a gift with horses and learning how to ride and rope from her father, Lucille was also a talented pianist and learned to appreciate the poetry of Robert Browning from her mother. She would have preferred to limit her education to her horses and riding across the more than five thousand acres of the Mulhall ranch, but her mother insisted she attend school. Before being enrolled at the St. Joseph Academy in Guthrie,

Oklahoma, Lucille attended a school at a convent in St. Louis, Missouri. Agnes had hoped her daughter would outgrow her desire to ride and spend all her free time practicing roping everything from a wolf to a steer and choose ball gowns, cotillions, and mid-afternoon teas with girls who preferred more refined tasks instead. Unfortunately for her mother, Lucille couldn't imagine herself anywhere except the wide-open range.[5]

Zack Mulhall encouraged Lucille's love of ranch life. She would accompany him to help with the cattle branding. She rode astride after the stray, wild steers hurrying away from the branding iron. Her father often boasted that she was equal to any two cowboys on the ranch in the measure of her ability and usefulness. When riding about the homestead, Lucille always carried a heavy pocketknife, a hammer and nails, and saddle tools. The hammer and nails were brought into use whenever she noticed a board loose in any of the fences about the ranch. Lucille was so good at maintaining the property and corralling runaway calves that her father made her a lucrative business proposition. For every yearling calf she roped and brought in, she could brand the animal with her own initials in order to build her own herd. The system worked well for a time, but Lucille's ambition increased with her skill, and her private herd kept pace with both. Zack rescinded the offer made to his daughter after he returned from a short trip and learned she'd roped and branded more than twenty of the finest and wildest steers on the ranch.[6]

Mulhall's Congress of Rough Riders and Ropers premiered at the St. Louis Fair in 1899. In addition to the bronc riders, steer ropers, and cowboy band members who performed in the program was a nineteen-year-old man from Oologah, Oklahoma, named Will Rogers. Will, or Billie as the Mulhall family called him, was the son of Clem Rogers, a wealthy Cherokee rancher and politician who was a friend of Lucille's father. Zack's association with Clem wasn't the only reason Will was invited to be part of the show. He was an exceptional trick and fancy roper and the winner of a highly competitive roping contest in Claremore, Oklahoma. Lucille was enamored with Will's talent. The two became fast friends, and she watched him practice for hours and learned his technique. In time, Lucille incorporated everything Will taught her about twirling a lasso into the act she presented in her father's popular exhibition.[7]

In addition to entertaining the crowds that flocked to the Wild West shows with her trick and fancy roping routine, Lucille played the part of a bandit holding up a stagecoach with a group of other wild riders. She enjoyed the work but wanted desperately to participate in the steer roping event with the boys. She pleaded with her father to give her a chance, reminding him of the calves she lassoed on the ranch. Zack felt his daughter was too young for such a challenge. Lucille would have to wait two more years before she could rope steers for an audience.[8]

An article in the May 17, 1901, edition of the *Pryor Creek Clipper* reported that fifteen-year-old Lucille Mulhall was scheduled to "take part in the contest of roping steer" on May 24, in Memphis, Tennessee. Among the other contestants participating in the event were professional cowboys Dick Parris, Clem Musgrove, and Will Rogers. Lucille would be the only female to compete. Although she didn't win any of the top prizes, she gave a respectable showing and proved to her father she could hold her own in the competition. Lucille rode and roped in other contests in Washington, D.C., and Des Moines, Iowa. Those events set the stage for her steer roping debut at the big carnival in El Paso, Texas.[9]

Promoters for the El Paso carnival were thrilled to announce that the "lady roper" had entered the roping contest. They anticipated Lucille's presence to be a big draw. "She has roped at the leading events of this kind all over the country," an article in the December 20, 1902, edition of the *El Paso Herald* noted, "and has never failed to make a hit or draw good crowds."[10]

Lucille traveled to the carnival with her brother Charley and her father. Under the direction of Zack Mulhall, the Mulhall Cowboy Band was performing at the festivities, and Charley was going to take part in the bronc riding competition. After the trio had settled into their hotel rooms, they took a tour of the rodeo grounds. Charley was taken aback by the fierce-looking steers selected for the event in which his sister was to take part. Lucille, however, was unphased and was looking forward to the challenge. Their father was more annoyed than worried for his daughter. Word had reached him that the oddsmakers were betting against Lucille. No one believed she could ride and throw a rope. Zack assured Lucille that he believed in her ability and was betting that the only woman competing in the steer roping event would finish on top.[11]

Lucille waited patiently on top of her horse, Robin, near the chute at the arena the day of the contest. When her name was announced, she moved into place at the starting line and gave her ride a pat on the neck. When the chute opened, the steer bolted out of the stall; Lucille urged Robin away from the starting line, and he raced after the animal. Lucille spun her lasso around quickly and tossed it out. The loop dropped down over the steer's horn, and the rope snapped in two. Charley was watching from the sidelines and, acting quickly, leaned over the fence around the arena and held out a fresh lasso. Lucille and Robin sped toward him, and Lucille grabbed the rope. As Robin hurried after the steer again, Lucille was spinning the lasso. In a flash, she flipped the loop over the steer's horns and placed the slack under the animal's right hip. The horse ran until the rope snapped tautly, then stopped and dug into the ground. The steer went down with a thud. Lucille jumped out of the saddle with the tie rope in her hands. She dropped to her knees next to the steer, and, with a quick flip, she wrapped the "piggin" strings around three legs and then got to her feet with her hands in the air.[12]

The crowd was cheering as the announcer proclaimed, "Lucille Mulhall, twenty-nine and a half seconds. Best time for the day!" The cheers and applause from the stands suddenly changed to shouts and screams. The spectators rushed toward the fence surrounding the arena, jumped over the barrier, and ran to Lucille. Before she knew what was happening, the crowd was pushing and grabbing at her and shouting that she was a man. The angry mob jerked at her blouse and pulled at her skirt in a harried attempt to find out if she was a woman. Lucille tried to break free from the crowd but was overwhelmed. Thankfully, her brother and father rode in on the scene with their horses. The crowd parted, and Charley grabbed his sister by the waist and hoisted her onto his mount, and the three hurried away.[13]

Newspapers from St. Louis to San Francisco reported on Lucille's performance. They called her the "Female Conqueror of Beef and Horn" and "The Ranch Queen." It was Will Rogers who gave her the name by which she would most be remembered. "Lucille was just a little kid when we began working together," Rogers recalled in his memoirs. "She was riding and running her pony all over the place…. It was the direct start of what has since come to be known as the cowgirl."[14]

Cowgirl Lucille Mulhall became a lead attraction in her father's Wild West show. With Lucille as the star, Mulhall's Congress of Rough Riders and Ropers was a highly sought-after rodeo. The group toured extensively through Colorado, Montana, Washington, and Texas. Billed as the "Champion Lady Rider and Roper of the World," Lucille was always competing, winning gold medals, belt buckles, and trophies for steer roping and cutting horses. She appreciated the attention she received as a woman competing in a man's sport and was humble and gracious. Reporters often remarked on her lack of vanity. "She has earned the title, wears it with delightful modesty, and is the idol of the cowboys throughout the country," the April 19, 1903, edition of the *Butte Miner* read. "At seventeen, she has the unique distinction of being the only professional woman ropist in the world, with sparkling jewels, by way of medal testimony, to bear witness to the fact. She has won these medals fairly and squarely in roping contests with the most skillful knights of the spur and lariat in Texas.[15]

"All men admire her grace, her courage and her dexterity, and all women envy her the possession of her equestrienne accomplishments. They admire her and envy her the more because they know that her pretty head cannot be turned by praise, nor her frank, girlish ingenuous and honest nature spoiled by the attention that she receives.[16]

"To lasso a steer running at full speed and throw and tie the struggling animal is not easy work for strong men who have spent most of their lives in the saddle. When a pretty, modest young woman rides with the same skill, throws a frantic steer, and ties him with the same dexterity, it is no wonder the world applauds….[17]

"Few women would have the courage to attempt roping, even if they had the strength and skill, as considerable danger accompanies such reckless riding.

"Miss Mulhall is the only woman ropist in the world recorded in cattle land. She is not the least masculine in appearance. So very girlish is she in looks and in manner that one would scarcely credit her with more than sixteen years."[18]

Lucille had many admirers, but her first allegiance was to her father and the rodeo. She didn't enter into a serious relationship until she was twenty-two years old and, even then, kept the romance a secret from the family. Zack often ran interference between his daughter and the young men interested in courting her. He was protective of Lucille and didn't want her settling down too soon.

In 1906, Mulhall's Congress of Rough Riders and Ropers disbanded. The show had become tiresome for many of its participants, and they decided to go in different directions. Lucille returned to the family ranch for a while, but she was soon lured back into show business by her father when an offer came for her to join a vaudeville review. The announcement of her return to the spotlight appeared in newspapers across the country. "Miss Lucille Mulhall's engagements will begin on January 20 in Orpheum at Kansas City where her father has completed a contract for her appearance in a number of cities," the January 18, 1907, edition of the *St. Louis Dispatch* noted. "The vaudeville act will be modeled after the Wild West shows in which she has taken part so often."[19]

Lucille's new show was billed as "Lucille Mulhall and Her Ranch Boys." In addition to Lucille, the troupe consisted of her two sisters, her brother, and a cowboy baritone named Martin Van Bergen. Several horses and props were a part of the entourage as well. Theaters had to be adapted to accommodate the show. A unique portable fence designed to hang from the fly loft and fasten between the stage and orchestra pit was installed in each venue. Several inches of dirt had to be spread out over the stage floor.[20]

Martin Van Bergen opened the show by riding out on a white horse and singing "My Lucille." During the song, a spotlight followed Lucille as she rode slowly across the back of the stage. At the end of the song, Martin would hurry off, and Lucille and Governor would then perform a variety of stunts.[21]

Lucille and Martin were smitten with each other from the start. He was impressed with Lucille's beauty and talent as a horsewoman. She fell in love with his appealing sweetness and captivating singing voice. The two were married on March 22, 1907.[22]

Their son, William Logan Van Bergen, was born on January 29, 1909. Lucille did not enjoy being a wife and mother. She planned to return to the rodeo program in the spring. She did, leaving her son in the care of his father and her in-laws. Her show played in every major city across the United States, and she spent so much time away from home that it took a toll on her marriage. Then her professional career began to falter.[23]

During a matinee show in Chicago, Lucille accidentally killed a steer in the arena, prompting the Society for the Prevention of Cruelty to Animals to press charges against her. "Several hundred men, women and children saw a badly frightened steer killed yesterday at the Coliseum by the woman roper, Lucille Mulhall," the May 19, 1910, edition of the *Chicago Livestock World* newspaper reported about the incident. "When the animal, struggling feebly as it was dragged about the ring by the young woman, gave a convulsive gasp and became unconscious, a cry of disgust and horror arose from the audience, and a dozen cowboys rushed forward and dragged the carcass from the arena...."[24]

"Lucille Mulhall, daughter of the proprietor of the show and herself noted as one of the best women ropers in the country, was giving her exhibition of roping a steer when the accident occurred. Usually during the conduct of the show, a small, well tamed steer has been selected for use in that part of the performance. The usual steer has been so accustomed to being roped that there was little of excitement to the act. Yesterday, however, a new steer was brought into the ring.

"Scared by the cries of the audience as well as by the strangeness of its surroundings, the steer darted about the arena at the coliseum until Miss Mulhall threw her rope at it.

"Instead of submitting to the roping as the property steer had been wont to do, the new animal started to break away. Miss Mulhall, seated upon her pony, tightened the noose, and in a moment the steer had fallen to the ground. As the steer was thrown to the ground, there came a sharp crack as if a bone had been broken, and the animal made a few convulsive kicks and then lay passive in the sawdust.

"...It was declared last night that members of the Humane Society would take action against the owners of the Wild West show in an effort to prevent a similar accident."[25]

A judge ultimately dismissed the charges against Lucille, but public opinion had turned against her. The incident wounded her reputation and promoted a state law against steer roping in Illinois.[26]

Hoping to distance herself from the bad publicity, Lucille abandoned her program and joined a troupe called California Frank's All Star Wild West Show. By 1911, she no longer spent any time with her husband or son. While with the troupe, she met an accomplished cowboy named Homer Wilson, and the two became romantically involved. William grew up knowing little about his mother. Martin had held out hope that Lucille's devotion would shift from rodeo life to domestic life, but it never happened. He filed for divorce on March 28, 1914. "Martin Van Bergen, baritone, and formerly a cowboy, has filed suit in Johnson County, Kansas, for a divorce from Lucille Mulhall (Van Bergen) charging desertion, and also naming Homer Wilson in other serious charges," an article in the March 31, 1914, edition of the *Manitoba Free Press* noted. "Mr. Van Bergen asks for custody of their son, William Logan Van Bergen, five years of age, living with his grandmother in Kansas.[27]

"The petition alleges that Miss Mulhall deserted the defendant over a year ago and has since been traveling about the country with a Wild West show in the company of Homer Wilson."[28]

Between theater engagements that same month, Lucille entered a roping contest in Walla Walla, Washington. She was twenty-eight years old and still quick with a lariat. Her best steer roping time was thirty-three seconds.* Her popularity was on the uprise, but it slowed down again when World War I sidetracked the nation. Still, Lucille continued to perform in rodeos and showed no sign of wanting to give up her profession, even if audience numbers weren't as high as they once had been.[29]

In 1919, she married a prominent cattle- and oilman named Thomas L. Burnett. She proved to be no better a wife the second time around, choosing again to travel with a rodeo she managed. Burnett filed for divorce two years later. The reason cited for the action was listed as "incompatibility." Lucille and Burnett's divorce was finalized in May 1922. She received $200,000 in cash and deeds to about five thousand acres of Texas land.[30]

From 1920 to 1930, Lucille continued to perform in both her own vaudeville productions and with established troupes like the Miller Brothers 101 Ranch Wild West show and the Passing of the West program.[31]

---

*By 1916, Lucille had graduated from being strictly a performer to producing her own Wild West show. Along with her business partner, Homer Wilson, the pair produced the first indoor rodeo at the coliseum building in Fort Worth, Texas. Lucille was the first female producer of Wild West shows.

In 1932, Lucille suffered several devastating blows. Her beloved parents died within less than a year of each other, and the Great Depression depleted the resources of the family ranch. Brokenhearted and in poor health, Lucille found herself living in poverty and turned to alcohol for solace. By the spring of 1935, she had pulled herself together and accepted an offer from her hometown of Guthrie, Oklahoma, to lead its annual Frontier Celebration Day parade. An excerpt from local newspaper reporter Noel Houston's column described the aging cowgirl's return to the saddle. "Once she was a vivacious, devil-may-care blonde in a divided skirt and white silk shirt as she passed in review before kings, presidents, and worshipping throngs," Houston's column read. "The thoughtless observer might see her now as only a gray, time-penciled old woman. But as she rode at the head of the frontier celebration in her traditional costume—beaded jacket over white silk waist, red corduroy skirt draping below her boot tops—Miss Mulhall was beautiful to me."[32]

Encouraged by the crowd's response to her parade appearance, Lucille agreed to join her brother's Wild West show. Now fifty years old, she participated only in special acts and didn't take part in the rodeos as a contestant. With her life and career back on track, she worked steadily, entertaining audiences and training horses. After more than forty years in the saddle, she was one of the most revered and fearless horsewomen in the world.[33]

On December 21, 1940, Lucille was on her way back to the family ranch when a truck broadsided the car she was riding in, killing her instantly. On a cold, rainy day, she was laid to rest alongside her parents. Few attended her graveside funeral. A notice in the December 27, 1940, edition of the *Daily Oklahoman* newspaper described the sad, somewhat ironic scene. "A machine killed Lucille Mulhall, but horses brought her to her final resting place," the article read. "So deep was the mud and so slippery the road, that a neighbor's plow horse had to pull the hearse from the highway to near the house, and the car bearing the relatives had to be pulled back to the highway after the service."[34]

Lucille received the greatest honor of her career in 1977, when she was inducted into the National Cowboy Hall of Fame. ❧

PART 2

BULLDOGGING

TILLIE BALDWIN
ONLY WOMAN BULL DOGGER IN THE WORLD

COPYRIGHT 1913
E.H.PAIGE

Mabel Strickland

Mabel Strickland stood a little over five feet tall, was slim, and was known by her friends and family to be as gentle as a dove. Few would have guessed by looking at her that she was a star in the rough, grueling sport of rodeo. Her name was held in high esteem at every big rodeo beginning in 1916, and thereafter for twenty-five years.

Not a specialist by any means, she participated in every competitive event on the rodeo bill except bulldogging. When you think of calves averaging 345 pounds giving well-muscled cowboys trouble, it is difficult to visualize tiny Mabel Strickland throwing a calf to the ground and pinning the flailing legs. Her fastest steer roping time was an impressive eighteen seconds.

She won the all-around cowgirl title at Cheyenne one year; then to prove herself she returned the following year and conquered every event she entered. In the 1920s, she was awarded two special Hamley saddles for her winning ways in relay races held at Pendleton and Cheyenne. She was also a trick riding expert and gave such exhibitions as jumping her horse over a car.

Legendary all-around cowgirl Mabel Strickland. PH244_0208, COURTESY OF THE UNIVERSITY OF OREGON.

Mabel was born in Walla Walla, Washington, in January 1899. She learned to ride at the same time she was learning to walk. She started her riding career in 1913 and first entered rodeo competition in 1916. She held top trick riding honors for ten years and appeared at Madison Square Garden rodeos numerous times. A spill there in 1926 almost ended her riding career. She was performing a trick in which she went under the horse's neck and grabbed the saddle on the other side as the horse galloped around the arena. She lost her grip and fell beneath the belly of the horse. It took several weeks, but she recovered and went on to win more riding honors.

Mabel's favorite riding horse was a quarter horse named Joker. Before he came into her possession, he belonged to a Texas sheriff who traveled the region with the animal tracking down outlaws. Joker took Mabel through more miles and rodeo wins than any other horse she owned.

Mabel passed away in 1979 after a long battle with cancer. She was seventy-nine years old. ⚜

Fox Hastings

Cowboy Bill Pickett is credited with introducing the sport of bulldogging to rodeos in 1907. In bulldogging, the rider dashes after a mad, fleeing steer, leans out from the saddle, throws himself onto the steer's horns, and brings the beast to the ground in a swirling scramble of dust and half a ton of flying beef. Often the steer is not thrown at once and there ensues a battle between the sharp-horned steer and the bare-handed rider until, if the rider wins, the steer lies prone.

Cowboys have been killed bulldogging, and for decades it has been considered one of the most dangerous stunts performed at rodeos. Early on, punchers had determined the daredevil event too hazardous for women to take part, but cowgirl Fox Hastings thought otherwise. At the Houston Stock Show in 1924, Fox became the first woman to tackle the event at that prestigious rodeo. She managed to bring the steer down in seventeen seconds.[35]

The strong young woman with nerves of steel learned the art of steer wrestling from the man who would become her husband, champion bulldogger Mike Hastings. Born in 1898 in Galt, California, Eloise Fox (aka Fox Hastings) was just fourteen years old when she decided she wanted to rope and ride. In 1912, she appeared at the state fair rodeo in Sacramento, competing in the bronc riding exhibition and in the quarter-mile sprint at the California Roundup. Finishing the race in thirty-two seconds, she and her horse placed third in the event.[36]

While appearing at rodeos from Reno, Nevada, to Cheyenne, Wyoming, she met a variety of influential people who doted on her talent. Not the least of those individuals was Charles Irwin. The Missouri-born rancher, rodeo cowboy, and showman established a Wild West show from his home in Wyoming that mirrored Buffalo Bill Cody's Wild West show. After witnessing Eloise's work in the saddle, he hired the teenager to be a regular in his program. Eloise was one of several cowgirls who gave daring riding exhibitions and demonstrations of her rope twirling skills.[37]

Charles Irwin wasn't the only one who saw something special in Eloise. Another member of the show's cast recognized the skill she possessed. Champion bulldogger Paul Raymond "Mike" Hastings noticed her fearlessness on the back of a wild bronc and was attracted to her courage and sense of adventure. Born in 1891 in Casper, Wyoming, Hastings, too, left home at an early age and joined the rodeo. The first rodeo in which he appeared was in 1910 in Laramie, Wyoming. In addition to bulldogging, he took part in the calf roping and bronc riding events. After teaching Eloise all he knew about steer wrestling, the pair wed in 1914. She then changed her name to Fox Hastings. The two competed in various contests in rodeos across the country. Mike set new records in the bulldogging sport, while Fox did the same in the categories for women such as bronc riding. She was billed as the "Bucking Horse Champion of Cheyenne."[38]

A turning point in Fox's career occurred in August 1916 at the New York Stampede at Sheepshead Bay Speedway in Brooklyn. Among the performers at the stampede was Bill Pickett. The fifty-year-old grandfather delivered an impressive exhibition of steer wrestling. Fox watched him ride his horse into the arena after the steer at neck-breaking speed. He jumped to the horns of the Texas steer and threw the animal in twenty-six seconds, the fastest time she'd ever seen. She appreciated all her husband had taught her about the sport and dreamed of combining the skill Mike had shown her with what she witnessed Pickett doing. She set her sights on becoming a bulldogger that day.[39]

In addition to the privilege of watching Bill Pickett work, the stampede at Sheepshead Bay Speedway was memorable to Fox for another reason. The number of rodeo stars scheduled to perform was staggering, and Fox was honored to be among them.[40]

Fox Hastings had nerves of steel and excelled at the sport of bull-dogging. DOUBLEDAY NEG. 204, WYOMING STATE ARCHIVES.

"All told, there were 350 in the party of Westerners, and today the second body will reach here, this party numbering 200," an article about the rodeo in the August 1, 1916, edition of the *Standard Union* read. "Traveling in two special trains, the participants for the world's championship in Western sports arrived over the Pennsylvania Railroad from Cheyenne. The first section was made up of the cowboys, cowgirls, and Indians. In the second section were the horses and cattle. These included 335 horses, wild outlaw animals, to be used in the wild horse races, 340 bucking horses, 250 horses for use in saddle entries and relay races, and 375 longhorn steers. All the animals were kept in the cars and taken by floats to Long Island City, and then by the Long Island Railroad to Sheepshead Bay, where they were put in corrals.[41]

"When the cowboys, cowgirls and Indians reached Manhattan, a parade up Broadway was started. They went to the stampede headquarters at Forty-ninth Street and Broadway where everyone registered. Among the cowboys were noted Scout Mash, who has won many bucking contests, Harry Walters, who lately won the bucking contest at Las Vegas, and Wild Bill Switzler, the champion roper. With the girls were Eloise Fox Hastings, the bucking horse champion of Cheyenne, Prairie Rose, also a bucking horse rider, and Edith Irwin, who is a noted rider in the West."[42]

In addition to participating in rodeos from Texas to Canada, Brooklyn to Sacramento, Fox and her husband had the privilege of performing for well-known actors, politicians, and even royalty. In July 1917, the couple took part in the Medicine Hat Stampede in Calgary. In attendance was the Prince of Wales and other members of the British Royal Family. The prince was a small boy, and he was in awe of the couple's talents. He requested and was granted a backstage visit with them, and Mike gave him a ride on his horse.[43]

In August 1923, the Hastingses appeared at the McCain Roundup in Barber County, Kansas. The annual rodeo event attracted spectators from Oklahoma and Colorado as well as Kansas. Fox performed a series of trick riding stunts and rode a couple of unruly horses in the bronc riding competition, finishing near the top of the contest. Mike demonstrated his bulldogging skills to the ticket buyers, winning top honors and the $100 purse. The Hastingses bunked in a tent on the hillside at night not far from the rodeo arena. In the evenings after the riding exhibitions, the pair would join the other competitors and townspeople on the dance floor, which featured a live band. During one of the dances, a trio of rowdy cowboys dared Fox to show them what her husband had taught her about steer wrestling. Mike stepped in, promising the men his wife was an exceptional bulldogger and telling them that in time she would show the community the extent of her talent.[44]

The question as to when Fox would indeed publicly attempt bulldogging followed her to the next rodeo in Joplin, Missouri, where she was to appear. According to the September 27, 1923, edition of the *Joplin Globe*, Fox told reporters that until meeting her husband she thought a bulldogger "was some kind of canine." Mike encouraged his wife to string the press along in order to build anticipation for the time she did wrestle a steer in an exhibition. From October 1923 to March 1924, Fox competed in trick riding and roping events with such high-profile cowgirls as Mable Strickland, Louise Hartwig, and Bea Kirnan. Everywhere she performed, she was asked about whether she would become a bulldogger. She was coy with her response, careful to give just enough information to keep reporters guessing.[45]

On March 22, 1924, Fox Hastings granted audiences at an exhibition in Houston, Texas, the first look at her skill in a sport relegated solely to men.

"Fox Hastings, the only woman who ever attempted to bulldog a steer, threw a brute of a steer this afternoon in twenty-seven seconds," a report in the March 24, 1924, edition of the *Galveston Daily News* noted. "She was slightly injured during the effort when the steer fell on her left leg. She had bruised the bone of her leg in one of her early trials last week, and since that time has been under care of a doctor, although she has bulldogged a steer in several of the rodeo performances.[46]

"This afternoon when she started after the steer, just as she was about to throw herself on its neck, the animal halted, and the woman was carried past. The steer was brought back, and she caught it in the second trial. The steer fell on her and hurt her leg, and she was unable to hold it down. The animal struggled back to its feet, but the injured woman hung on, and in a last burst of strength, downed it."[47]

Fox wrestled her next steer at a privately staged rodeo in Fort Worth, Texas, on April 15, 1924. The woman bulldogger pulled the animal down in forty-six seconds. She then signed a contract with the Shrine Club Rodeo to repeat the daring feat at an event in Bristow, Oklahoma, in May and at the Tri-State Roundup in July in South Dakota. Billed as the "only lady bulldogger," the June 7, 1924, edition of the *Daily Deadwood Pioneer Times* reported that she "mounts one of the fastest horses and speeds out in pursuit of the longhorn, leaps from the saddle, grasping the bovine by the horns and in a short but desperate hand to horn battle, subdues a wild steer many times her own weight, throwing the animal prone upon the ground.[48]

"This 138-pound Western girl has made history in rodeo sports, has proven that a life in the open and in the saddle brings superhuman strength. Picture if you will, a girl of this weight riding like the wind in pursuit of a wild and vicious longhorn, making a flying leap from the back of her cowpony to the head and horns of an infuriated steer and grasping the animal by the horns and engaging in a fierce wrestling match, pitting her skill and courage against vicious cunning and brute strength of an eight hundred pound steer, and you have an idea of the courage and daring of the Western girl who has recently launched into the daring sport of bulldogging."[49]

The dangers of the sport caught up with Fox in July 1924. She broke her leg bulldogging, and that break kept her out of the rodeo arena for more than ten weeks. If she recovered in time, she was expected to appear at the North of 36 Rodeo in Houston, Texas, in September. Fox did recover and managed to participate in the event, breaking the steer's horns in the process. Before the end of the year, the fearless rider would become the first woman to bulldog at a major rodeo. In time, Fox ceased to be a mere novelty. She didn't get killed or lose her nerve, and her bulldogging record became a chronicle of fast throws without a miss. While waiting in the chute before an exhibition, Fox told reporters, "If I can just get my fanny out of the saddle and my feet planted, there's not a steer that can last against me."[50]

From Texas, Fox traveled to New York to ride in Tex Austin's Rodeo at Madison Square Garden, then on to the Pendleton Roundup in Oregon, the DeMolay's World Championship Cowboy Contest in Kansas City, and the Tucson Rodeo in Tucson, Arizona.[51]

The first time Fox competed in a bulldogging event against men was in early March 1925 at the Southwestern Exposition and Fat Stock Show in Fort Worth, Texas. "No favoritism will be shown to this cowgirl," an article in the February 10, 1925, edition of the *Vernon Record* read. "Fox Hastings will be given a fair chance to do her stuff. The popular rodeo star is the young lady who will powder her nose then fling herself from the back of her charging bronc into the horns of a swiftly moving steer."[52]

The coliseum where the exposition was held, located in the heart of the Fort Worth Stockyard, was jammed with spectators the afternoon of the event. More than six thousand enthusiastic rodeo fans scrambled to find a place to sit inside the arena, and many were turned away due to the lack of seats. "Save for a creditable bulldogging of a steer by Fox Hastings, announced as the 'only lady bulldogger in the world,' the steers and broncs probably came out with the palm for the afternoon," the March 11, 1925, edition of the *Fort Worth Star-Telegram* announced. "And Lady Fox herself was winded completely after a long tussle with the unchivalrous steer, though she was given a warm ovation."[53]

Fox was in great demand after the Fort Worth event. She was recognized from coast to coast as an entertainer who could "produce one of the biggest thrills of all whenever she appears on a rodeo program and goes about the business of conquering a steer ten times her weight."[54] Newspaper reporters clamored for interviews with Fox, following her into any setting for a chance to speak with her. On July 24, 1925, she welcomed journalists into her hospital room in Wichita, Kansas.[55]

"Fox Hastings, a slip of a girl who comes from way out West where women are women, is the heroine of the hour wherever riders and ropers gather for a rodeo," a reporter with the *Ardmore Daily Press* later wrote about his time with the bulldogger. "The reason is a painful exhibition of courageous grit she gave during the rodeo here. Fox was given the title of the 'world's champion cowgirl' at the last rodeo in Madison Square Garden, New York. A marvelous rider, she gives thrilling exhibitions of steer bulldogging that make women scream and the men grow pale, her admirers say.[56]

"In leaping from her horse to grab a steer's horns, she hit the ground with her leg twisted up under her, and the limb was broken. Despite this, she downed and tied up the raging steer in the record time of 10 seconds. Then she arose to her feet, waved at the awed crowd with a smile, and crumpled to the ground in a faint.

"She is in a local hospital, very unhappy, because she must stay in bed while the rodeo season is at its height. It will be months, doctors say, before she can dare to try to ride anymore wild bulls. But Fox is willing to try it with her leg in bandages."[57]

The injury that led to Fox's hospital stay happened at a rodeo in Wichita, Kansas. It kept her from appearing at events where patrons had pre-purchased tickets just to see her. Rodeo organizers scrambled to line up other attractions they hoped would be just as thrilling, but many ticket buyers demanded their money back if Fox was not going to be there.[58]

By late fall 1925, Fox was back at work participating in rodeos from Florida to California. At the Ascot Park Rodeo in Los Angeles in October, Fox was once again forced to withdraw from the bulldogging event due to an injury. A steer trampled on her in front of the grandstands and rendered her unconscious.[59]

The itinerant lady bulldogger returned to competition in March 1926, appearing once again at the Southwestern Exposition and Fat Stock Show in Fort Worth. Fox brought the crowd, who gathered to watch the rodeo, howling to its feet when she downed a burly steer in 9.45 seconds.[60]

With such an incredible time, Fox's career soared even more than it had before. She continued to participate in all the major rodeos on the circuit, thrilling audiences with her strength and agility. "When I see that old steer come charging down the track," she told a correspondent with the *Coweta Times Star* in Oklahoma, "I almost shudder with fright. But in a moment, it is all over. I leap from my horse and make a catch for the steer's horns. Then there is the tussle to pull the steer's neck over and finally after I am successful the tonic of the applause from the grandstands."[61]

At the age of twenty-eight, Fox Hastings was a cowgirl in high demand. According to the July 4, 1926, edition of the *Philadelphia Inquirer*, her "bravery and daring" were the source of her popularity. "Bulldogging, or steer wrestling, which even the cow country regards as too hazardous for their women folk, requires tremendous strength, superb daring and as much skill as any outdoor sport, and Fox Hastings excels in the sport," the article read. "When a man weighing 150 pounds tackles and throws a running steer weighing in the neighborhood of a half a ton, he must have developed all three combined with perfect coordination of hand and brain. Yet Fox Hastings, weighing just 140 pounds, beat all records established by men competitors.[62]

"Two cowgirls, two horses, and one bull are required for the bulldogging act. One of the mounted girls is Miss Hastings, the other her assistant, or known otherwise as a hazer. The bull is released from the chute between the two riders and immediately tears out at top speed down the field. A length to the rear on the right gallops the assistant, whose sole duty is to keep the bull from swerving from her direction. Then up from the rear tears Miss Hastings. At the instant she is almost abreast of the running steer, she hurls herself from the saddle to grasp the horns of the animal. If successful in making the leap, she swings her feet ahead of the bull, and when the latter's head comes down the doggers' feet are dug into the ground to act as a break to bring the steer to a stop. Then slowly but surely the bull's head is twisted until he drops to the ground. Fox then throws up her hands, and the throw is considered complete.[63]

"Few spectators can stay in their seats after watching her work. They jump to their feet applauding."[64]

Fox's bulldogging profession flourished, but her marriage to Mike Hastings began faltering in mid-1927. He was jealous of her continued success and threatened by the younger male riders competing in the sport. Mike was arrested for assaulting up-and-coming bulldogger Bob Belcher at a rodeo at Madison Square Garden on November 2, 1927. Belcher's wife, cowgirl Claire Belcher, accused Mike of putting oil of mustard on a steer she was bulldogging, causing her to be thrown and breaking two ribs. Mike denied the act when confronted by Belcher and then punched Belcher in the eye when the man insisted his "time in the sport was over." Mike was fined $5 by the court and instructed to "get his temper under control." Fox would complain later he wasn't able to do as the judge ordered and that over time, he grew more and more belligerent at home.[65]

Mike and Fox's marriage limped along until the summer of 1929. The pair separated shortly after his prize bulldogging horse, Stranger, died. When the divorce was finalized, Fox began dating a nationally known rodeo star from Kansas named Charlie Wilson. The two were married on October 23, 1929, in Manhattan, New York.[66]

Fox maintained her rodeo career after she married Charlie, but, for the first time in years, her interests extended beyond bulldogging. She wanted to be an aviatrix. In an interview with a reporter for the *El Paso Evening Post*, Fox shared that she had always been fascinated with planes and flying and that she wasn't afraid of the idea of piloting a small engine craft. She admitted to being truly afraid only once in her life. "I was in Juarez competing in a rodeo when a man came up to me in the Keno Hall and tried to put his arm around me," she told the newspaper reporter. "When I had knocked him down the third time, the police arrested me and took me, fighting, to the police station. I thought I was going to spend the night in jail, but my friends intervened in time."[67]

The Wilsons made their home in Winslow, Arizona, and the two rode the rodeo circuit together from 1930 to 1935. In January 1936, Fox was hospitalized in Tucson, Arizona. The illness with which she was suffering forced her to withdraw from competitions scheduled for the first half of the year.[68] In an interview with the *Napa Journal*, Fox let the public know she was anxious to bulldog again and assured readers that when feeling well she'd "much rather tackle a steer than a broom."[69]

Fox spent twenty years of her life following the rodeo circuit. She had been tossed from horse to horn and had suffered concussions, broken legs, crushed ribs, and fractured arms. "I wouldn't give this up for any other life," she told the *Napa Journal* reporter. "I like the thrill when I match my 135 pounds against a half ton of brute force. I like the feeling of triumph which surges through me when the animal falls to the ground."[70]

Fox recovered briefly from the illness that kept her out of the arena in early 1936. When the illness was determined to be tuberculosis, she gave up the rodeo and returned to her home in Arizona where Charlie devoted himself to her care.[71]

On July 30, 1948, Charlie died of a heart attack. He was forty-nine years old. Fox was devastated. Less than three months after Charlie's death, the grieving widow decided to take her own life. Fox died of a self-inflicted gunshot wound. Her body was found in a room she had rented at Hotel Adams in Phoenix. According to the August 15, 1948, edition of the *Arizona Republic*, Fox left a note behind that read, "I don't want to live without my husband."[72]

Eloise Fox Hastings Wilson was fifty when she died.

The red-headed wrestler of longhorn steers tackled her job as daringly as the most skilled cowpuncher. When she was inducted into the Cowboy Hall of Fame in 1987, Fox was celebrated not only for bulldogging, but bronc riding and trick riding as well. ❧

PART 3

BRONC RIDING

Mildred Douglas

When twenty-four-year-old Mildred Douglas rode a steer in the Garden City, Kansas, rodeo in 1919, it was a big deal. Never before had a woman ever ridden a steer in competition, but Douglas was no ordinary woman. Born in Philadelphia on August 21, 1895, Mildred knew at the age of seven what she wanted to be when she grew up. Her parents had taken her to the Barnum & Bailey Circus in Franklin Field in Pennsylvania, and she sat at the end of a row where she could look over the canvas and see the animals and performers coming in. Mildred knew she had to be part of such a show and work with animals of all kinds. She dedicated herself to making her dream come true. At the age of twenty-two, she won the title of "World Champion Girl Bronc Rider," was proficient as a trick rider and shooter, and was destined for stardom in the type of shows she saw as a child.

Though Mildred May Douglas was a champion bronc rider and a star of Wild West shows, she wasn't born to the life of a cowgirl roughrider. According to the National Cowgirl Museum and Hall of Fame in Fort Worth, Mildred Douglas left an East Coast finishing school to join the 101 Ranch Wild West

Though Mildred May Douglas was a champion bronc rider and a star of Wild West shows, she wasn't born to the life of a cowgirl roughrider. DOUBLEDAY NEG. 181, WYOMING STATE ARCHIVES.

show. She spent years touring the country in rodeos, circuses, and other popular Western shows.

Mildred met her first husband, Pat Chrisman, while performing with the 101 Ranch Wild West show. Pat was a horse trainer for silent film star Tom Mix's ride. Mildred was captivated with motion pictures. Her fascination for the medium, along with her incredible talent and versatility in the saddle, led to a studio contract. Mildred was hired to appear in several films with Tom Mix himself. In addition to her onscreen duties, Mildred trained and worked with horses, lions, leopards, and other animals scheduled to appear in motion pictures and in circuses.

Pat Chrisman died in 1953, and Mildred then decided to pursue another dream she'd had—that of becoming a nurse. At the age of fifty-nine, she officially entered the profession and took a position at the Comanche County Memorial Hospital in Lawton, Oklahoma. In 1954, she traded in her fringed leather riding outfits for a white uniform and a starched nurse's cap. Her life as a Wild West performer was never far from her mind, however. She often brought her scrapbooks to the hospital and showed photographs from her other life to interested coworkers and patients. She always spoke fondly of the animals she trained and the audiences she entertained. Mildred eventually donated those scrapbooks, saddles, movie photos, rawhide ropes, and other memorabilia to the Museum of the Great Plains in Lawton, Oklahoma.

Mildred Douglas Chrisman died in September 1982 at the age of eighty-seven. She was inducted into the National Cowgirl Museum and Hall of Fame in 1988. ✢

Kitty Canutt

Bronc busting champion Kitty Wilkes won her first title at the Wild West Celebration Rodeo in Miles City, Montana, in 1916. The seventeen-year-old, New York native's straightforwardness and untamed physical daring gave fans the impression she was born and bred into the rugged life of a Wyoming ranch. Few would have guessed she was new to the sport or that winning the top prize would inspire her to excel in other rodeos. From that exciting moment in Miles City she was determined to show the world that one need not be "born in the saddle" to be a crack rider.

Katherine Derre, whose stage name was Kitty Wilkes, was born on July 15, 1899. She had a natural talent for breaking horses and parlayed that skill into bronc riding in public showings. Not only did she have a way with wild horses, but she was also an exceptional trick and fancy rider. Owners of relay strings were eager to gain her services.

Between the rodeo in Montana in the summer of 1916 and the Pendleton Roundup in Pendleton,

Kitty Canutt was determined to show the world that one need not be "born in the saddle" to be a crack rider. MEYERS *4182,* B916/04182, *WYOMING STATE ARCHIVES.*

Oregon, in early fall of 1916, Kitty honed her bronc riding talent at ranches and rodeos throughout the West. She insisted on using the orneriest animals for training. Outlaw horses were blindfolded and saddled for her to ride. One encounter resulted in the horse bucking Kitty off and bruising her ribs. She wouldn't allow the horse to beat her, however. She swung back into the saddle, refusing to leave it until the animal finally broke.

Kitty's nickname was Diamond Girl because she had a diamond set in her front tooth. When needed, she would remove the diamond and pawn it for the entry fees to rodeo contests.

Her performance at the Pendleton Roundup in 1916 resulted in her being named "All-Around Champion Cowgirl." Among the many people she met during the roundup was Yakima Canutt. Canutt, who also competed at the rodeo, would go on to become one of Hollywood's leading stuntmen. Kitty and Yakima fell in love and were married in Kalispell, Montana, in 1917.

Kitty was a fierce athlete who hated to lose. It was not uncommon for her to challenge women who outrode her, and she believed cheated, to a fistfight. In September 1918, she was disqualified from participating in a rodeo in Washington because she hit a rider in the mouth with a piece of wood.

Not content with being the top female bronc rider in the country, she aspired to be the top female relay racer as well. Rodeo fans loved to watch the petite woman fly past the grandstands on her horse, hurrying to meet the next mount waiting to be saddled and ridden to the next point. More than once Kitty would be finishing part of the race standing on the stirrups trying to get into the saddle. Her grit and resolve often paid off with a win.

The rodeo stars Kitty often competed against were Mabel Strickland, Bonnie McCarroll, and Prairie Rose Henderson.

Kitty Canutt was eighty-eight years old when she died on June 3, 1988. ❧

Prairie Rose Henderson

On March 1, 1933, four men left Casper, Wyoming, to search for a woman who had been missing since mid-February. Mrs. Rose Coleman was reported missing by her husband, the reputed cattle rustler Charles W. Coleman. Charles wrote his brother-in-law Ernest Gale from jail informing him that he'd not heard from his wife for more than two weeks and was worried. Gale recruited three of his friends to travel to the Green Mountains, fifty miles northwest of Rawlins, to look for his sister. The Colemans' ranch was in that area, and it was the last place Charles saw his wife when he was arrested on February 10, 1933.[73]

Ernest and the other men traipsed through deep snowdrifts around the Colemans' home and into the dense forest surrounding the property but found no trace of the woman.[74]

News of Rose Coleman's disappearance made headlines in all the Wyoming newspapers. Reporters speculated she left the state carrying with her incriminating evidence against her husband. Charged with stealing and slaughtering cattle, authorities believed he had several accomplices and that his wife might have been one of them. It was well known that Rose was devoted to Charles, and the idea she would assist him in a crime or try to hide his misdeeds was not unreasonable.[75]

More than a month after the search began, and subsequently halted due to blizzard-like conditions, Rose had still not been seen. In early April, state law enforcement commissioner George Smith received an anonymous call from a man claiming to have met her in Riverton where she was staying with a friend. Smith told the press he had sent officers to the location to talk with her, but the authorities could not confirm she was, indeed, in town. There was a rumor she had left the state and was living in California.[76]

Charles was convicted and sent to the state prison. Law enforcement officers returned to the Coleman ranch in late spring when the snow began to melt to search again for Rose. The woman was still nowhere to be found, and there were no clues to help authorities determine what might have happened to her.[77]

If the police knew the missing Rose Coleman was also known as Prairie Rose Henderson, they did not note it in their records. There was nothing written to tie her to the days when she was a rodeo star. Even the newspapers glossed over that fact. More than two decades had passed since she burst onto the scene riding wild horses, and all that had been forgotten.

Rose Coleman was born on February 5, 1875, in Ohio. Her parents, Ezra and Melvina Gale, named their little girl Rose Belle. When her father passed away in 1883, mother and daughter moved to Nebraska to be close to her mother's brothers and sisters. Melvina remarried, and she and her new husband had three sons.[78]

Rose was married several times. Her first husband, Arthur Columbus Clayton, and she were married in Custer County, Nebraska, in September 1893. In three short years, the couple had two children, a daughter named Cora May and a son named Henry Arthur. When exactly Rose took an interest in riding is unclear. By the time the Claytons' son was born in January 1896, the pair was living in Sweetwater, Wyoming.[79]

The first annual Frontier Days celebration was held in Cheyenne in September 1897. According to the October 14, 1897, edition of the *Natrona County Tribune*, "the purpose of the event was to perpetuate the memory of the sturdy pioneers who settled in the wilderness and became founders of a new state." Included in the celebration was a program where working cowboys put their ranching skills to the test by competing against one another for prizes in roping and riding. Rose decided to show off her talent for racing horses at Frontier Days in 1899. Arthur also took part in festivities roping steers.[80]

More than 117 years ago, the first cowgirl bronc rider whose name was Prairie Rose Henderson, competed in the Cheyenne Frontier Days. z-641, THE DENVER PUBLIC LIBRARY, SPECIAL COLLECTIONS.

Not long after participating in the Frontier Days event, the Claytons moved to Clarksville, Nebraska. By 1906, Rose and Arthur had divorced, and Rose relocated with her children to a town close to Salt Lake City in Utah. Whether in Nebraska or Utah, Rose continued to hone her riding talent. There are some reports that note Rose competed in women's cow pony races in Denver, Colorado, and in Highland Boy, Utah, and even won trophies for the event; however, there is no concrete evidence to support the claim.[81]

At some point prior to 1910, Rose signed on with Charles and Frank Irwin's Wild West show. The Irwins had been instrumental in orchestrating Cheyenne's Frontier Days but, after a few years, had decided to create their own show and take it on the road. Rose was one of the first women hired to be a part of their program. She successfully parlayed the survival skills she learned riding and working on the prairie into a sport on the rodeo grounds. While employed with the Irwin Brothers Wild West Show, she met a bulldogger named Tom Henderson. Henderson had once been a working cowboy on a Colorado ranch, and he was married to lady rider Maude Tarr. Rose and Tom became romantically involved, and she adopted his last name. By 1910, she was being billed as Prairie Rose Henderson. Prairie Rose was primarily a bronc rider, but she also participated in roping and trick riding events.[82]

Prairie Rose officially burst onto the rodeo scene in El Paso, Texas, in March 1912 when she dared to ride a famous outlaw horse named Kelly. The wild bucking bronco had thrown and trampled numerous cowboys. Rose would be the first woman to try and stay on the animal's back for a record-breaking time. After conquering Kelly, she volunteered to ride another unbroken beast named Dynamite Powers. At the end of the Cowboy Park Rodeo, Rose had won more than $100 in prize money.[83]

From Texas, she hurried to California to appear in the Los Angeles Rodeo. She entered the women's roping contest and competed against Bertha Blanchett and Hazel Hoxie. Next, Rose made her way to Wyoming to participate once again in the Frontier Days celebrations. The world championship bronco busting honors were at stake in Cheyenne. Rose and Goldie St. Clair were each determined to carry off the woman's title. St. Clair had won the competition in 1911, but Rose was expected to outride her in the 1912 contest. Riding the horse Gin Fiz, Rose gave a respectable showing and, after four days of competition, was named the winner and new champion.[84]

Rose took little time out to celebrate her big win. The cast of the Irwin Brothers Wild West Show was expected in Topeka, Kansas. She performed before a packed crowd riding a renegade horse named Bowman. According to the September 12, 1912, edition of the *Topeka Daily Capitol*, Bowman was the least of Rose's worries during the riding exhibition. Clouds of giant green bugs filled the arena, swarmed around the entertainers, and, at times, made it hard for Rose to see. The insects kept her from performing at her best.[85]

When Prairie Rose Henderson entered the Los Angeles Rodeo in February 1913, she took home the top prize in the bucking horse contest. Not long after winning the title, she learned she would be competing against Fanny Sperry Steele at Frontier Days in Cheyenne. Fanny had been named "Lady Bucking Horse Champion of the World" at the Calgary Stampede, and Rose was determined to hold on to the title at the contest in Wyoming in July. A $500 purse was on the line.[86]

Rodeo fans appreciated Rose both for her ability to stick in the saddle and for how she dressed during the ride. Rose's look was unique. She wore Turkish-style pants that gathered just below the knees, chiffon blouses, and vests covered with sequins, feathers, or furs. Newspaper reporters interviewing her about her riding talents would inevitably ask her about her costumes and what she thought of the everchanging fashions of the day. "'Prairie Rose' Henderson, although a wearer of the split skirt, is not an apostle of the cause of revolution in women's dress," an article in the July 3, 1913, edition of the *Sioux City Journal* noted. "I can see nothing commendable in the split skirt, and even dislike the riding skirt, although riding is my specialty. Out here in camp I'm always looking ahead to the period of free time in which I can put on what I consider a proper skirt. Camp life and companionship with the rangers makes one careless, but I never seem to get away from a desire to be like other women."[87]

Sadly, Rose did not win the women's bronc riding contest at Frontier Days. Her relationship with Tom Henderson was suffering, and she later admitted to being preoccupied with thoughts about their future. Unable to prevent what she believed to be the "ultimate demise" of her association with the cowboy, she focused on performing in the Wild West show. The Irwin Brothers troupe met in Wisconsin in late July 1913 to present an exhibit at the state fair. Rose received top billing among the cowgirls with the program, and *Frank Leslie's Illustrated Newspaper* featured Rose on the cover of the July 21 edition of the publication.[88]

In August, Rose was in Canada and in an exhibition at the Calgary Stampede with Hazel Walker, Blanche McGaughey, and Fanny Sperry Steele. At the conclusion of the program, Rose returned to her home in Utah. With the relationship between her and Tom Henderson dissolved, she could focus solely on her children and her new romantic interest, an engineer named Homer Corwin. Except for participating in the Pendleton Roundup in Oregon and Frontier Days in Walla Walla, Washington, in September 1914, winning the cowgirl's bucking contest in the Washington rodeo, Rose stayed close to home.[89]

On November 2, 1914, Rose and Homer were married in Salt Lake City.[90]

Rose's rodeo name did not change when she wed Corwin. Prairie Rose Henderson was known throughout the rodeo circuit as the "Ladies' Bronc Busting Champion." A three-reel Western roundup motion picture featuring the well-known rider was shown in nickelodeons from coast to coast in 1915. Her popularity attracted crowds, but it didn't guarantee she would maintain the bronc riding title she had worked so hard to obtain. Dorothy Morrell took the top prize in that category in May 1915 at the Roundup Rodeo in Cheyenne. Rose vowed to improve and take the next title.[91]

As always, in between competing in rodeos, Rose performed in the Irwin Brothers' shows. On October 5, 1915, Rose appeared at a Wild West show in Salt Lake and participated in a cow pony race against Mrs. Roy Rogers of St. Anthony, Idaho, and Mrs. Theone Hampshire of Salt Lake. Although Mrs. Rogers contested the results, Prairie Rose beat both riders to the finish line.[92]

From 1916 to 1918, Rose stayed true to participating in the most popular rodeos, including Walla Walla Frontier Days, the American Royal Livestock Show, and the Pendleton Roundup. She consistently placed in the top three or five women vying for bucking championship awards and many times won top honors. Wherever Rose rode and won bucking titles, she received prize money along with either a trophy or belt buckle, and sometimes both. Everywhere she appeared, rodeo fans crowded the stadium to see the "cowgirl with the reputation for skill and daring subduing bucking broncos" and to admire the items she was awarded.[93]

Tragedy struck Rose and her family in early 1919 when her twenty-four-year-old daughter Cora died suddenly. An inquest was conducted to confirm the cause of death. Authorities deemed it necessary because at the time Cora passed away she was a patient of a chiropractor whose medical practice was called into question. She had sought his services because she was suffering from what she thought was a pulled muscle in her back. She stopped seeing the doctor when she wasn't getting any better and checked herself into a hospital. Authorities suspected the chiropractor's treatments might have contributed to her demise. A full investigation was conducted, and it was concluded that Cora died from the Spanish flu.[94]

Rose returned to the rodeo arena the summer after her daughter's death to perform at the First Annual Roundup in Indianapolis. Among the other noted female performers at the event were Fox Hastings, Mayme Stroud, Maude Tarr, and Mildred Douglas. Rose was billed as the "greatest woman bronc buster in the country" and was praised for having won more championships than any other lady rider in the world.[95]

Between the summers of 1919 and 1925, she defended her titles or fought to gain them back. She sustained a few injuries in the process, some more serious than others. On September 29, 1920, the bronc she was riding at the annual Pawnee County Fair and Roundup in Larned, Kansas, broke loose and ran into the trees at the corner of the rodeo grounds. Rose was trying to get the horse under control when her head met a limb and two of her front teeth were knocked out.[96]

Somewhere between rodeos, Rose and her husband Homer separated and then divorced. Shortly after that marriage ended, she met and married a trick roper from Los Angeles named Johnny Judd. The pair were introduced by the producers of the silent picture *Cowboy Jazz*. Both Rose and Johnny were in the film along with several other well-known rodeo performers such as Ruth Roach and Tommy Kirnan. After the premiere of *Cowboy Jazz* in the fall of 1920, the Judds spent the winter in Hollywood working as stunt riders in Western star William S. Hart films.[97]

Although Rose's interests now included motion pictures, she didn't abandon the rodeo. She continued to compete in bronc riding contests from Oregon to New York. At fifty years old, she appeared at the Frontier Roundup in Salt Lake in 1925 to ride against familiar challengers Lily Allen, Marie Gibson, and Bonnie Gray. The Utah event was the last time Rose participated in a rodeo. After that, she drifted from competition and from her marriage to Judd at the same time. The couple divorced, and she moved to Wyoming where she met her next husband, Charles Coleman.[98]

Rose and Charles were married on August 29, 1929, in Lander, Wyoming. The couple settled on a ranch near Rawlins. Authorities would later note the "Coleman home was in one of the most secluded and isolated spots in that section of the West." Fremont County officers who had dealt with Coleman speculated he selected the property because he could "hide his illegal activities there." Coleman was a thief when he and Rose married, and he wasn't particular about what kind of livestock he stole. The week before their wedding, he had been caught on rancher Henry Johnson's land looking over the forty thousand head of sheep he owned. Johnson fired two shots at Coleman to scare him away. Coleman reported Johnson's action to the sheriff, and the rancher was arrested.[99]

When Coleman was apprehended in February 1933 in connection with cattle rustling, the sheriff's department assured Rose they would return with provisions for her. A heavy snow had blanketed the region, and another storm had been forecasted. The officers were concerned Rose might be trapped at the ranch and unable to get food. True to their word, law enforcement officials came back with groceries, but Rose wasn't at home.[100]

A search was immediately instituted, but efforts to find the rodeo star were hampered by bad weather. The fact that Rose had deserted pets of which she was quite fond and that her brother hadn't heard from her led residents in Lander to believe she had become lost in the snow or met with an accident.

On Sunday, July 22, 1939, Mrs. Rose Coleman was finally located. A sheepherder named A. Martinez happened upon her remains less than two and a half miles from the Coleman ranch. Rose's brother returned to Rawlins to identify her skeleton and clothing. She was wearing one of the belt buckles she had won busting broncos.[101]

Three months after her body was found, Prairie Rose Henderson was laid to rest at the Lakeview Cemetery in Cheyenne.[102] ◄

PART 4

TRICK SHOOTING

Pearl Biron

The crowd attending the John Robinson's Circus in Clarksdale, Mississippi, swelled around the rodeo arena where expert equestrienne, roper, and whip cracker Pearl Biron was performing. Twenty-six year old Pearl was the master of the Australian bullwhip. She could flick the ashes off the cigarette of a fellow performer or a flag off the head of her horse. Pearl had traveled to Australia early in her career to learn how to use the heavy whip designed for mustering cattle. From atop her roan, she could crack the whip through strategically placed targets and flick a row of balls off posts around the stadium. Audiences across the country marveled at her exceptional talent.

Pearl Biron was born in Maine in 1902 and, while she was in her late teens, became a skilled horseback rider and master of the bullwhip. Often billed as the "sweetheart of the rodeo," Pearl was beautiful as well as clever. She appeared in the arena of a variety of shows including the George V. Adams Rodeo and Col. T. Johnson's Championship Rodeo.

Pearl was often paired with rodeo circus clown Cherokee Hammond. Pearl would demonstrate her trick riding skills around Cherokee and his mule, Piccolo Pete. In their nightly performances, Cherokee and Piccolo Pete would play a prospector and his ride heading off to the gold rush. In the show, when the pair found itself attacked by Indians, Pearl and her horse would ride in to save the day. Critics praised the routine as "thrilling" and "one that spectators thoroughly enjoyed."

Pearl also won honors for fancy roping and trick horseback riding at

Pearl Biron was often referred to as the "Sweetheart of the rodeo." COURTESY OF COWGIRL MAGAZINE.

Madison Square Garden in New York and at similar rodeo competitions in Dallas, Texas, and Cheyenne, Wyoming. In 1940, she was billed as the "World's Champion Trick Rider."

The beautiful rodeo performer received standing ovations for her signature trick performed at the close of her time in the arena. Enthusiastic fans selected from the audience would tear sheets of paper in half and give them to members of the rodeo troupe to hold in their mouths. Pearl would ride past the brave members of the troupe and snap the paper out of their teeth with the flick of her whip.

Pearl married Dan H. Biron of Arizona, and the couple made a home for themselves and their son in Chandler. Dan was a foreman on a guest ranch, and, when Pearl retired from the rodeo, the couple worked together. Pearl would teach guests how to ride and would dazzle them with her bullwhip skills at night around the campfire.

Pearl Biron passed away in 1978 at the age of seventy-six. ✦

May Manning Lillie

A bespectacled photographer emerged from under a black curtain draped over a massive camera and tripod. In his right hand he held an instrument that when pressed would take a picture. In his left hand he held a flash attachment to illuminate his subject. "On the count of three, Mrs. Lillie," he warned. May Manning Lillie stared directly into the lens. Her cowboy hat sat cocked on her head, a red kerchief was tied around the neck of her white peasant blouse, a black split skirt was belted around her waist, and leather gauntlets covered her hands. She wore a serious expression as the photographer began counting. Before he got to two, she raised a six-shooter and pointed it at the camera. One eye was closed, and the other looked down the barrel of the gun. Ka-Poof! The flash attachment fired, and smoke wafted into the air. "Perfect," the photographer said, smiling, and it was. The black-and-white image of cowgirl May demonstrating her skill as a marksman became one of the most widely publicized Wild West posters in the early 1900s.

May's life as a trick rider and shooter in Wild West shows was far from the lifestyle in which she was raised. Born in March 1869 in Philadelphia to Dr. William R. Manning, a prominent physician, and his wife and aide, Mary, May and her family were Quakers. They were quiet, unassuming people, reluctant to draw attention to themselves. If not for a chance meeting with frontiersman and performer Gordon William Lillie at a Buffalo Bill Cody Wild West show in Philadelphia in 1885, May might have married a modest man from her faith, never venturing far from her birthplace. Lillie, better known as Pawnee Bill, was a twenty-six-year-old Pawnee Indian interpreter who was smitten with May the moment he saw her.[103]

"I was standing on the show grounds in front of the main tent when May came by," Lillie later recalled in his memoirs. "She was a schoolgirl then and carried her books under her arm. I thought I noticed her smile, and I turned and tipped my hat. She thought I was funny with my long hair, sombrero, and buckskin clothes, and just laughed out loud."[104]

May was a student at Smith College who was home visiting her family for the summer. She attended Cody's Wild West show with her sister. Lillie sent a note to May letting her know he'd like to meet her. The two formally introduced themselves to one another after the program concluded. Lillie learned seventeen-year old May was studying to earn a Bachelor of Arts degree, and May learned Lillie was a former teacher and Commissioner of Indian Affairs. "It was love at first sight and I knew she was the girl for me," Lillie noted in his memoirs.[105]

Although May was charmed by Lillie, her parents were immune, at least at first. He had walked May home the night they met, and it was only after they arrived at the Mannings' house that he realized the doctor and his wife were hosting a dinner party. May's mother and father were not pleased their daughter had brought a cowboy home. Lillie tried to fit in and spent time talking with the guests about the West. Most had the impression that Native Americans were wandering the frontier massacring white settlers. Lillie gently explained they were wrong and briefly shared what he knew of the Indians' plight. He forgot to exercise good manners during the exchange and spit on the floor. May's father and mother were mortified by his behavior and urged her to see Lillie out of their house.[106]

May returned to college and Lillie to the Wild West show. The two wrote one another often. A year after their first meeting, Lillie confessed his love for her and proposed. May graduated college in the spring of 1886, and she and Lillie married on August 31 of that same year. Lillie had assured Dr. Manning he would be providing for his daughter with the earnings he made performing in the Wild West shows and from his cattle ranch in Kansas. Despite Lillie's long hair and strange buckskin-fringed clothing, which was another source of concern for the Mannings, the doctor and Mary gave the union their blessing. The Mannings arranged the ceremony that was attended by numerous friends and family. The September 1, 1886, edition of the *Evening Telegram* reported that "a Quaker girl in pigtails was given in marriage, at Siloam Church to Gordon W. Lillie, of the plains country."[107]

Not long after the ceremony, the Lillies boarded a train bound for his ranch in Wellington, Kansas. May was apprehensive about the move at first. She'd never been West and worried she'd have a hard time adjusting to her new home. Sensing her concern, Lillie telegraphed his friends when to expect them and to make their arrival something special for his bride. According to Lillie's memoirs, "Fifty or sixty gentlemen and ladies turned out with a band to receive us and gave us a serenade." Lillie's sister held a reception for the newlyweds to celebrate their marriage and introduce May to the family and townspeople.[108]

May was happy to be married to Lillie, and, although everyone went out of their way to make her feel welcome, she didn't feel she belonged on a ranch. Lillie traveled a great deal with the Wild West show, and she was left alone. She found work at the local bank and kept herself busy decorating their home, but it didn't stop her from being homesick. In October 1886, she learned she was going to have a baby. Planning for the new arrival helped alleviate the loneliness, but the tragic event that would change her life was not far off.[109]

"In the natural course of events, a baby boy came to us in June 1887," May wrote in her journal. "Gordon was away. Babies were important only to the immediate parties most concerned in those days, so a country midwife was the only hope and consolation at the blessed event.[110]

"I was proud of my ten-and-a-half-pound son, and, when Gordon rushed home to see us three days after his birth, I foolishly arose from my bed to greet the proud father. The consequences of that rash act were terrible. To add to my suffering, our son lived only six weeks.

"A serious operation was necessary for me to correct complications which caused recurring illness."[111]

The surgical procedure May underwent left her unable to have any more children. She was devastated and, for several weeks, was too despondent to leave the house. From her bedroom window, she sat and watched the daily activities at the ranch. Oddly enough, it eventually provided her with the inspiration to move beyond the sorrow and find a reason to go on.[112]

When May finally felt well enough to leave her home, she made her way to the paddock to visit with the cowboys breaking the horses on her husband's ranch. Lillie and the ranch hands taught May how to ride and to shoot. "She cultivated a taste for the rifle," Lillie wrote in his memoirs, "and at her first shooting match carried off the laurels by missing the object not a single time." May practiced her newfound talent constantly. By the fall of 1887, she had joined Lillie on the road and become part of the Wild West show. The September 16, 1887, edition of the *Peabody Weekly Republican* reported on one of May's first performances. "Pawnee Bill and his famous Indian scouts and cowboys were, undoubtedly, the drawing cards this season," the article began. "Mr. G. William Lillie, is the United States of Pawnee Bill's name, and the daring lady equestrienne rifle shot and heroine of the plains—May Lillie—was introduced to us as his wife. We found her to be all that is advertised on the bills and a perfect lady besides, educated and refined."[113]

May charmed crowds and the press in every city she appeared. An article in the December 10, 1887, edition of the *Boston Journal* expressed the depth of feeling for the budding equestrienne and performer. "She took to them [cattle and horses] as most girls gravitate to ballrooms and pink teas. When her classmates were debutantes, entering upon the social whirl of conventional life, she was learning the tricks of the lariat. While they were making conquests of city hearts, she was roping steers and study-ing the art of remaining comfortable on the hurricane deck of a bucking mustang. Her recitals and soirees became target matches with the rifle and six-shooter. She brought the entire culture of the East into the cow camps of the West, and she exchanged her beneficent influence for the skill of her new companions."[114]

The Pawnee Indians who lived near the Lillies' ranch were also impressed with May's riding ability. To show their admiration for her skill and kindness to them, they gifted her with a colt she named Hunter. Hunter and May were inseparable. She rode him at an exhibition at the Pennsylvania State Rifle Range on November 12, 1887. In addition to demonstrating how well Hunter could perform various tricks, May participated in the shooting com-

May Manning Lillie, also known as the "Princess of the Prairie," overcame personal tragedy to become the star of Pawnee Bill's Wild West show. BUFFALO BILL CENTER OF THE WEST, CODY, WYOMING: MCCRACKEN RESEARCH LIBRARY; MS071 MERCALDO COLLECTION; P.71.657

petition. The months of practice she put in paid off in a big way. Shooting at two hundred yards, she scored twenty-four points out of a possible twenty-five. It was the best score ever made by a woman at that distance. May was presented with a gold medal inscribed, "Presented to May Lillie Champion Girl Shot of the West."[115]

In the spring of 1888, Lillie organized his own Wild West program and made May one of the stars of the show. She continued to be well received by audiences, and newspaper reviews of her performances called the feisty equestrienne the "Princess of the Prairie." Her proficiency with a rifle earned her the additional title of the "New Rifle Queen." People who flocked to Pawnee Bill's Historical Wild West show to see May were never disappointed. "Her work with the rifle is extraordinary," an article in the August 7, 1889, edition of the *Ashland Weekly News* read. "She is the only woman in the world able to break targets thrown in the air while riding at full speed on her mustang."[116]

The Lillies toured the United States and Europe for more than twenty years performing for audiences of all types, including politicians and royalty. "It is remarkable that May Manning Lillie, bride, learned the show business, became an expert rifle shot, and was known as a champion horseback rider and marksman, one of the features of the show," an article in the January 15, 1928, edition of the *Oakland Tribune* read. "...She is known throughout America for her skill as an expert shot and was one of the chief attractions with her husband's show, and later the combined shows of Buffalo Bill and Pawnee Bill. When not on the road, the Lillies make their home at Blue Hawk Peak, near the town of Pawnee, Oklahoma."[117]

Pawnee Bill's Wild West show was a triumph in every respect, especially financially. May was not only responsible for the success of the show as a performer, but also contributed to its success behind the scenes as well. With May's exceptional business and money management skills, the couple was able to invest in many profitable ventures, including a two-thousand-acre buffalo sanctuary in southwest Oklahoma. Lillie and May didn't agree on every investment, particularly one he made on his own in 1908. Lillie purchased James Bailey's (of Barnum & Bailey fame) interest in Buffalo Bill Cody's Wild West show. Lillie and Cody then decided to merge their popular programs and renamed the Western exhibition Buffalo Bill's Wild West and Pawnee Bill's Great Far East. May was against the merger. She believed Cody to be a poor businessman. She felt he overspent on everything for his shows.[118]

Throughout the many years May performed with the Wild West shows, the public remained fascinated with her daring accomplishments. Women wanted to know about her upbringing, her life as an equestrienne celebrity, and what advice she might have for those with a desire to be a trick rider and shooter. May addressed all those queries in an interview with the *Joliet News* on June 6, 1907. "Miss Lillie was born in the East but, when still a child, went West with her parents and remained there until budding womanhood, when she returned East to complete her education," the article read. "While her European experience in school served to polish off the rough edges of

Western life, it did not remove the self-reliance and confidence acquired in her Western home. Her early love for horses and horseback riding remained. The time that other women give to household and social affairs, Miss Lillie devoted to her horse, and her happiest hours were spent in the saddle. She never was happier than when off for a twenty-mile dash across the prairie or assisting in a roundup of cattle. She has roped and broke horses that men of greater experience would hesitate to approach.[119]

"She adds to her native talent, courage, determination and love of her art, and endows her public performances with charming grace and finish of manner, movement and method. Her equestrienne accomplishments range from simple to complex and from artistic and polite to intrepidly rough. No equine spirit is too wild or purpose too savage for her to quench and rule. She is an equestrienne empress whose throne is in her saddle and whose four-footed subjects are her devoted pride.[120]

"The apotheosis of high school revelations is seen in Miss Lillie's quartet of prize-winning steeds. Guided solely by the voice and gesture of their fair trainer, they executed a multiplicity of exacting feats that illustrate the extreme possibilities in equine expositions. Beyond this extraordinary performance it is impossible to go."[121]

According to May, "Let any normally healthy woman who is ordinarily strong screw up her courage and tackle a bucking bronco, and she will find the most fascinating pastime in the field of feminine athletic endeavor. There is nothing to compare to increase the joy of living, and, once accomplished, she'll have more real fun than any pink tea or theatre party or ballroom every yielded."[122]

May retired from Lillie's Wild West show with Cody in the mid-1910s. She decided then to shift her focus from performing to growing the buffalo ranch she and Lillie had purchased on Blue Hawk Peak in Pawnee, Oklahoma. Despite her protest, May was never completely removed from the "Two Bills" program. Photographs of her graced playbills and posters exhibited throughout the West. In addition to overseeing the daily operations at the ranch, May became active in church and community services, including the National Women's Relief Corp and Auxiliary to the Grand Army of the Republic.[123]

In December 1916, May and Lillie traveled to Kansas City to adopt a four-year-old boy they named Billy. Sadly, the boy died in a tragic accident at the ranch in 1925. May fought through the devastating loss by caring for the buffalo and other livestock.[124]

On August 31, 1936, May and Lillie celebrated their fiftieth wedding anniversary. To commemorate the special event, the couple decided to renew their vows. The special event was held in Taos, New Mexico. More than five hundred guests and spectators attended the ceremony.

"Pawnee Bill, the Indian scout and showman, wore the same buckskin suit he wore at the first marriage, but his wife dressed in an Alice blue gown of lace, with turban to match and silver slippers," the August 31, 1936, edition of the *El Reno Daily Tribune* read. "Preceding the ceremony on the plaza of old Taos, a tribe of Indians from a nearby reservation, twelve flower girls in Spanish attire, and scores of tourists assembled. Lillie recalled his long and nearly frustrated romance with the daughter of stern Quaker parents in Pennsylvania.[125]

"They met on a sidewalk in front of a theatre in Philadelphia where Pawnee Bill was appearing in the Wild West show headed by William F. Buffalo Bill Cody. Their first reaction, Lillie said, was that each looked twice. 'I thought she was the prettiest girl I ever saw, and I haven't changed my thought,' the white-haired Indian fighter said. 'My first thought when I saw Pawnee Bill,' Mrs. Lillie remarked, 'was what a funny man.' Lillie coughed and glowered at his aged wife, then said he was 'sorry I taught May so much about shooting irons.'"[126]

Less than two weeks after the golden wedding anniversary celebration, Lillie and May were driving back to their home in Oklahoma when they were involved in a head-on collision. They were both seriously injured. May's injuries proved fatal.[127]

May Manning Lillie was laid to rest at the Highland Cemetery in the Pawnee Indian hills of Pawnee, Oklahoma. She was sixty-seven years old. Her memory lives on in the popular photograph she posed for when she was best known as the "New Rifle Queen."[128] ❧

PART 5

HOBBLED STIRRUP RIDING

Peggy Warren

On Saturday, July 1, 1916, at the Passing of the West rodeo in Butte, Montana, it appeared all the wild, outlaw horses had been saved for the lady riders. It took cowboys ten minutes to corral and saddle the cantankerous animal cowgirl Peggy Warren was to ride. The horse reared and bucked, kicked and plunged, and fought against the harness and the blind. When Peggy finally climbed onto his back and raced out of the chute, the horse threw himself backwards in a vicious lunge. In a masterful display of grit and determination, Peggy held on and stayed in the saddle despite the horse's extraordinary exhibition of bucking. It was that kind of bold riding that earned Peggy the reputation for being one of the most daring equestriennes of the West.

Born Hazel Agnes Wedderien in California in September 1889, Peggy learned to ride at an early age, and, by the time she was in her late teens, she was recognized as an expert hobbled stirrup rider. She was fearless on the back of a horse. She could ride standing in the saddle, a trick known as the hippodrome; and balance on one foot and perform death-defying tricks such as the Death Drag, a trick where the rider hangs upside down from her horse.

Peggy Warren had a reputation for being one of the most daring equestriennes of the West. PH036_3365, COURTESY OF THE UNIVERSITY OF OREGON.

Between 1912 and 1916, Peggy participated in the Pendleton Roundup, the Calgary Stampede, the Winnipeg Stampede, and the Los Angeles Rodeo. In addition to bronco busting, she competed in relay and pony races. From atop her horse Babe Lee, Peggy dazzled audiences with her fast riding and trick roping.

She was married twice and began her career using her first husband's name. Billed as Hazel Walker, she performed alongside other celebrated female rodeo stars such as Fanny Sperry Steele, Lucille Mulhall, and Vera McGinnis. Her second husband was first-class bulldogger Frank Warren. After the pair wed, Hazel changed her name to Peggy Warren.

Peggy won numerous rodeo championships, sustaining more than a few injuries along the way. She was the victim of many sprained ankles, fractured ribs, and broken wrists. One of her most serious injuries occurred in October 1916 at a rodeo in Great Falls, Montana, while participating in an event called the "race for a bride." Peggy was in the lead, but in no time other riders caught up to her. As the riders flanked her on either side her horse spooked, stumbled, fell, and rolled on top of her. She was left unconscious on the ground. "Any ride can end badly," Peggy later remarked to a reporter at the *Great Falls Tribune*. "If nothing is broken, you shake it off and get back in the race as fast as you can."

Peggy Warren retired from rodeo riding in the early 1920s and lived out the rest of her life with her family in Garfield County, Washington. ◄

Goldie St. Clair

High-spirited Goldie St. Clair, champion girl bucking horse rider of the world, rode with several other cowgirls in the street parade to the rodeo grounds where the 101 Ranch Wild West show was going to be performing in Scranton, Pennsylvania, in June 1911. A year prior, Goldie had captured the bronco riding title at the Frontier Days celebration in Cheyenne, Wyoming. She rode an outlaw horse named Red Bird that did some terrific bucking but was unable to unseat its rider. Among the crowd watching her demonstration of skill and nerve that day was former president Roosevelt.

At the conclusion of the event, he gallantly summoned her to his box so he could congratulate her on the ride.

Irene (Goldie) Wooden was born in Kansas in 1890, but she grew up on a ranch in Maramec, Oklahoma. There, she learned to ride some of the most cantankerous horses on the cattle farm. Naturally modest and quiet, she was anything but that on the back of a horse. By the age of fourteen, she was winning fame as a rider in the Miller Brothers 101 Ranch Wild West show. She traveled the country working for the 101 Ranch and Buffalo Bill Cody's show.

In 1907, Goldie competed in a bucking horse competition at the Jamestown Exposition and World's Fair in Jamestown, Virginia. It was there she won a gold medal and title of "Lady Bucking Horse Rider of the World." In the spring of 1908, Goldie was hired to ride for Dickey's Circle D Ranch Wild West Show in Milwaukee. During the sixteen weeks she worked for Will A. Dickey, she performed most every week, sometimes giving up to eight performances a day. The male bronc riders with the show would only agree to ride bucking broncs twice a day. Rodeo fans came often to see the fierce teenage rider with a rugged brand of showmanship.

All-around cowgirl champion Goldie St. Clair had an unmistakable style in riding, roping, and dress. COURTESY OF COWGIRL MAGAZINE.

While with the Dickey show, Goldie met and married her first husband, fellow performer Burney St. Clair. After they were married, the couple continued with the Dickey show until it closed.

Cowboy humorist Will Rogers sought out Goldie not long after she won the bronc riding title at the Frontier Days show in Wyoming. He signed Goldie and her husband to a six-week contract to perform on Broadway. Standing at the side of the stage while going through his roping act, Will Rogers would keep up a continual patter about the talented women in his troupe. Some of the gifted lady ropers would then join him on stage and perform a few tricks. The act closed with Goldie riding a bucking horse.

Goldie competed in the first Calgary Stampede in 1912 and held the women's bronc riding title of the world for several years.

Goldie and Burney divorced in 1929; shortly afterward she married a rancher named Tom Hillis. She retired from bronc riding and managed a ranch in Alberta, Canada, with her new husband. Goldie died on November 30, 1956, from injuries she sustained in a car accident. She was sixty-six years old. ❦

Tillie Baldwin

Hundreds of rodeo fans filled every available seat at the Pendleton Roundup in northwestern Oregon in late September 1912. They cheered loudly for Norwegian bronc buster Tillie Baldwin sitting atop an outlaw horse named Spike. The gate was moments away from opening, and the bronc was already bucking wildly. Tillie ground her hat down tightly on her head and then clenched the thick reins of her ride. The chute opened, and Spike darted out into the arena. Holding on with all her might, Tillie bobbed up and down in the saddle as the horse worked violently to try and throw her off his back. At long last, a horn sounded, and the ride was officially over. Tillie had survived the long trek around the arena on top an animal that had been unsuccessful in tossing her to the ground. The crowd enthusiastically applauded the twenty-four-year-old, and the remarkable ride earned her first prize in the women's bucking bronco contest. She was awarded a $350 saddle. In addition to winning the bucking

Tillie Baldwin was not only an exceptional all-around rider and bulldogger, but she also excelled at trick riding. PH036_3599, COURTESY OF THE UNIVERSITY OF OREGON.

bronco championship, Tillie also won the trick riding competition and its $150 purse.[129]

Tillie Baldwin was born Anna Mathilda Winger in Arendal, Norway, in 1888. She was fourteen years old when she immigrated to the United States with her family in 1902, and she did not speak English. Six years later, she had mastered the language and become a hairdresser with a healthy clientele of New York ladies wanting a new look.[130]

Tillie made friends easily, and the group of young women she spent time with enjoyed regular trips to Staten Island. One day, there was a troupe of actors near the beach where the ladies liked to visit. The actors were busy making a film. The movie in which the cowboys and cowgirls were appearing was titled *Red Wing and Young Deer*.* Tillie and her friends were mesmerized by the wonderful costumes and what seemed like the colorful lives of the actors and actresses. The teenage hairdresser immediately wanted to learn to ride a horse and join the troupe. Tillie returned to New York after the outing with a dream she couldn't shake. She wanted to ride a horse like Young Deer and decided to return to Staten Island to talk with cast members about her ambition. Tillie offered to pay one of the cowboy actors to teach her to ride. The pair worked for weeks, and eventually she morphed into a competent

The husband-and-wife team who were the leads in the film were members of the Winnebago tribe in Nebraska who starred in one-reel Westerns during the first part of the silent film era.

equestrienne. She learned how to ride and perform a couple of tricks in the saddle, including snatching up a handkerchief lying on the ground.[131]

Shortly after learning to ride and perform additional tricks, Tillie approached the producer of the film and asked if she could join the cast. He agreed, and she was paid $6 a week for her efforts. From silent pictures, the eager young woman signed a contract to join Captain Jack Baldwin's Western show. There, she perfected her riding skills, met her husband Johnny Baldwin, and changed her name from Mathilda Winger to Tillie Baldwin.[132]

Tillie's big break came months later when she met Will Rogers. The cowboy humorist was passing through the city en route to Philadelphia where he was to give an exhibition at the National League baseball park. Tillie took advantage of the chance encounter and shared with the stage actor that she was a trick rider. Rogers hired her to perform with him in Philadelphia. Tillie remained with Rogers' program until the Miller Brothers 101 Ranch Wild West show visited Brooklyn.[133]

It was while watching the parade of entertainers marching down New York Avenue that Tillie made up her mind to join the cast of the Miller Brothers' show. Just as she had been swept away by the costumes and impressive men and women seated tall in their saddles preparing to be filmed, she was awestruck by the horses and riders in the 101 Ranch Wild West show. Without a moment's hesitation, Tillie approached Joseph Miller, one of the show's producers, and informed him that she wanted to sign up with his show as a trick rider. Miller appreciated her boldness but wanted her to give a demonstration of what she could do.[134]

It was a rainy day, but Tillie wasn't going to let the weather keep her from showing off all she'd learned. She borrowed a horse from one of the show's cast members and performed many of her tricks. Miller thought Tillie had talent and invited her to be part of the program. Tillie was with the 101 Ranch Wild West show for two seasons. During that time, she became more and more proficient at trick riding and went on to learn about bronc busting and bulldogging.[135]

After Tillie's success at the Pendleton Roundup in 1912, she decided to concentrate on her rodeo career. From Oregon, she traveled to southern California to participate in the International Rodeo in February 1913.

The world's champion woman bronco buster attracted a large audience, and she did not disappoint patrons wanting to see her add to her title. Tillie was named best woman rider at the Los Angeles event, as well as top cowgirl trick rider.[136]

In between rodeos, the celebrated equestrienne appeared in a few stampede shows. A stampede show features more acts and riders than a rodeo. Riders can win trophies, medals, or other prizes, but their participation is more an exhibition of their skill than a competition. In early July 1913, Tillie agreed to ride some of the wildest horses known on the stampede circuit. She also took part in the woman's relay pony race. In such a race, the women rode one horse one lap around the track, switched to another horse for a second lap, rode a third horse for the final lap, and sprinted to the finish line. Tillie won the woman's relay race at the Tacoma Stampede in Tacoma, Washington, on July 3, 1913. At the Winnipeg Stampede in Winnipeg, Manitoba, Canada, in August 1913, Tillie won the trick and fancy riding event, the Roman standing race,** and gave a bulldogging exhibition. Tillie told reporters with the *Spokesman Review* that she was a real cowgirl and she was going to wrestle a steer to prove it. She practiced for the event on a tame, half-breed cow, but when it came to the actual performance, she used a steer from the Texas longhorns at the stampede.[137]

Newspapers and advertisements across the country heralded the notoriety of Tillie Baldwin. Her daring feats inside the rodeo arena had made her well known, but, according to her friends and family, that fame didn't change her at all. She held tightly to her conservative values, refusing to drink or engage in any questionable behavior. As male fans sat in clubs, hotels, and at home in the early hours of the morning and smoked gilt-wrapped cigars bearing the picture of Tillie Baldwin, Tillie was sleeping soundly, conserving her strength for the next day's riding schedule. While the smokers of the night before were soundly sleeping the next morning, Tillie was beginning her next day's program because she was a firm believer and follower of the early to bed and early to rise theory.

In September 1916, the former New York hairdresser, who had defeated the best cowgirls in the country and won bronc busting and rough riding championship contests, shared her secret for capturing those titles.

** *Roman riding is when a rider stands with each foot on the back of a pair of horses.*

"Bronco-busting depends mainly on the knee-grip," she told a reporter with *The Times* on September 9, 1916. "You hold on with the lower part of the thigh, being careful to keep the legs curved in, so that the calves cling to the animal's flanks. And you don't try to sit erect in your saddle. I lean back and keep my chin down so that when the animal bucks he doesn't jerk my head back and hurt my neck.[138]

"For straight racing, such as we do in the relays, you naturally need a different seat. Then you stand in your stirrups, cling with the knees only, and bend the body over the horse's neck. That's the jockey seat. I guess that's about all there is to riding except practice and lots of strength."[139]

When Tillie wasn't riding in rodeos or stampede shows, she lent her talent to county fairs. She and her husband would give exhibitions of rough riding and perform death-defying tricks atop their horses. The couple had settled in Connecticut, and many of the carnivals and fairs they took part in were close to their home. Tillie enjoyed life in New London, a coastal town that overlooks the Thames River, but she preferred being on the road competing.[140]

The Calgary Stampede, held in August 1919, provided Tillie with the perfect opportunity to show off her riding skills, earn a top spot in the festivities, and take a shot at a piece of the $25,000 cash prize. One of the contests she entered was the women's bulldogging event. Tillie was prepared for the competition, but the steer was not. It wanted nothing to do with the performance and fought to get back to the corral. "Cornered by horsemen, it [the steer] made three escapes over the fence of the enclosure, and at one time tried to find a place in the boxes among the audience," a report in the August 28, 1919, edition of the *Calgary Herald* read. "Another animal was procured and Tillie, leaping from the back of her grey mount, put the huge black beast down in splendid style and very good time."[141]

At rodeos and stampedes where Tillie appeared in 1920, she was routinely billed as the "fearless rider who had never been thrown from a bucking bronco." More than a decade after entering the profession, she continued to astonish crowds with her clever riding. In June 1921, rodeo fans from coast to coast named Tillie Baldwin, along with Fanny Sperry, and Bertha Blanchett, as three of the best women riders in the country.[142]

By 1925, Tillie had retired from rodeo competitions, divorced John Baldwin, and married William C. Slate, a landowner residing in South Lyme, Connecticut. She might have been out of the bronc busting spotlight, but neither the press nor her fans had forgotten the champion equestrienne.[143]

"It was not more than two years ago that the name, Tillie Baldwin, glittered upon the horizon of fame," an article in the August 23, 1925, edition of the *Hartford Courant* about the lady bronc buster began. "Only yesterday did the critics spread far and wide the story of her success. Jammed were the curbs of many cities, while spectators awaited the approach of her bespangled figure as she smartly reined her pony through their ranks on circus day.[144]

"Large and glaring were the posters advertising the coming show and featuring Tillie Baldwin, fearless, intrepid, rough rider horsewoman. Throughout the West and in some sections of the East gentlemen were pleased to select from plate-glass showcases, cigars labelled 'Let em, buck,' encircled in wrappers of gilt with a picture of Tillie Baldwin on either side.

"And then the curtain dropped upon the colorful career of Miss Baldwin. The shrill and enthusiastic cries for 'Tillie' softened, and the hoofs of her pony were not heard at anymore stampedes. Not that the proficiency of this buxom girl is not spoken of now or that she at present does not hold a role in life as important as she did then—but today she is far from the eyes of her admiring world as she enjoys the peaceful seclusion of her beautiful home in Connecticut.[145]

"Remarkable enough is the record of her deeds, which for a woman have seldom been equaled and in one instance never excelled. Almost unbelievable are the authentic reports of the many mad bulls she has wrestled with, finally throwing the powerful animals to the earth. But for Anna Mathilda Winger, a lass from Norway and later a New York hairdresser, her achievements, embracing stunts too much for girls, natives of the Golden West are as yet unsurpassed.

"But the West claims Tillie Baldwin as its own. And the West has a good claim for it was there that Tillie became a cowgirl, and it was in the land of the cattle and trails that she won her spurs. The West is the land she loves and there is no disputing that she is a real rider of the West.[146]

"Her home is typical of the West. It resembles a ranch house in appearance with circular driveway in back. Many valuable saddles, weapons, Indian trinkets, a beaded vest, bridles, broad brimmed hats, and boots adorn the wall of the Slate residence. Often, Mrs. Slate becomes Tillie Baldwin for the time, and she may be seen dashing about the country on her pony, of which she is maintaining several at present.

"Almost daily she passed with the throng in a nearby city. There is no semblance of the cowgirl in this tall and finely dressed woman. A lone medal attached to a ribbon, which she generally wears, is the only way one might learn that Mrs. Slate is Tillie Baldwin, broncho buster, buckaroo, and trick rider of note."[147]

Tillie retired from the professional rodeo world but not from riding. She took a job as manager of the Fred Stone Ranch*** in East Lyme. Stone sold his interest in the ranch in 1931, and the land was taken over by the government. Tillie stayed on as caretaker. It is said that Tillie would not tolerate rough stuff from the cowhands about the ranch. In an article in the August 18, 1957, edition of the *Hartford Courant*, Tillie laughingly recalled a couple of "boys," Mike and Ike, who were always raising Cain when they drank too much. "One day they got on my nerves," she explained, "and I picked them up and heaved them bodily out of the bunk house. You never saw two more sheepish and surprised fellows in your life."[148]

In 1932, Tillie opened her own riding school in South Lyme, Connecticut. She owned more than thirty horses and enjoyed teaching aspiring equestrians the art of trick roping and good horsemanship.[149]

When Will Rogers died on August 15, 1935, Connecticut newspapers, who knew of Tillie's one-time professional relationship with him, sought her out for an interview. She was distressed over his passing and explained to reporters that the reason she won the world championship at Pendleton, Oregon, in 1912, was because of his training. "I can't believe he's gone," she remarked. "Rogers was a frequent visitor at the ranch, and we always enjoyed his company."[150]

Tillie made the news again in August 1936 when she applied for a job as the first and only policewoman in New London, Connecticut. The former cowgirl assured the police chief that since she could handle a wild steer she

---

*** *Fred Stone was a musical comedy actor.*

ought to be able to throw any ordinary roughneck. "There's no doubt that I am fitted for the job," she told reporters for the *Daily News*. "In show business a girl meets a certain number of men who are not so gentlemanly. She has got to learn to handle herself. I always managed to do so. I never had to ask for anyone to fight my battles for me. A capable and fearless woman can handle any situation as well as a man, if she has training."[151]

Tillie's application was ultimately denied.

Tillie returned to the rodeo arena for a special presentation in September 1946. She appeared at Madison Square Garden along with Frank Biron, the men's world champion trick rider.[152]

Tillie spent her later years in life painting and hosting exhibits of her work. The rodeo star died on October 23, 1958. She had been suffering with a heart ailment and passed away at the New London hospital. She was seventy years old.[153] ◄

PART 6

TRICK RIDING

Bonnie Gray

From the early 1920s to the mid-1930s, trick and fancy rider Bonnie Gray and her company were recognized as some of the best rodeo performers in the country. The famous, all-around cowgirl solidified her place in the profession as an expert in the "under-the-belly crawl" stunt. Riding quickly into the arena atop her horse, King Tut, Bonnie would drop down on the nearside of the horse, feed herself headfirst between the animal's galloping legs, reach through, haul herself up the off side, and jump back into the saddle again. Audiences from Manhattan to Cheyenne were dazzled by the skill and daring it took to execute the death-defying trick.

Bonnie Jean Gray was a natural athlete. Born in Kettle Falls, Washington, in 1891, she learned to ride on her family's ranch. She was also a gifted musician. An accomplished pianist, she attended the University of Idaho

BONNIE GRAY GOING UNDER HER HORSE
(DOUBLEDAY)

Bonnie Gray was a trick rider best known for her "under-the-belly-crawl" stunt. DOUBLEDAY NEG. *179, WYOMING STATE ARCHIVES.*

where she majored in music and participated in a variety of sports including track and tennis.

Among her many other abilities, Bonnie had a talent for medicine. During World War I, she studied nursing at a military post in Montana. She used her nursing expertise assisting her brother who was a doctor in Arizona. She helped deliver many babies and tended to those struck down with influenza in 1917 and 1918.

Bonnie's interest in trick riding was something she'd had since she was a little girl. She decided to pursue the sport in 1918 and, in 1922, made her professional debut. She participated in some of the biggest rodeos across the country and in Canada. In a short time, she had earned the title of "World's Champion Woman Rider."

According to the February 23, 1923, edition of the *Deming Headlight*, Bonnie had charmed the fans by her overall look and attracted attention as the only woman to have ridden bulls used in the bullfights in Mexico. "Is she pretty?" the article posed. "Yes, in a softly, feminine way, with a row of dazzling white teeth that show no traces of dental adornment. She's fearless in the saddle as well as beautiful."

In June 1930, Bonnie married trick rider Donald Harris in Los Angeles, California. The bridal party was on horseback, and the ceremony was held in an elaborately decorated arena with more than a hundred mounted guests in attendance.

Bonnie and Donald's marriage was a volatile one. Donald was physically abusive, and, by August 1932, the couple was divorced.

After the divorce was finalized, Bonnie left the rodeo world to become a motion picture stuntwoman. She doubled for popular Western film stars Tom Mix, Tim McCoy, Hoot Gibson, and Ken Maynard. One of the most elaborate and dangerous stunts she performed on camera involved her and the horse the studio had her ride. The pair jumped a clump of brush and hurtled down a ten-foot cliff. Bonnie was paid $10,000 for the stunt, but vowed she'd never agree to participate in anything else so hazardous again.

Bonnie Gray Harris died on April 28, 1988, at the age of ninety-seven. She is buried at Forest Lawn Memorial Park in Hollywood Hills, California. ✦

Florence LaDue

Twenty-nine-year-old Florence LaDue laid on her back in the middle of a rodeo arena in Alberta, Canada, twirling a lasso. It was July 1910, and the crowd in the stands watching her work were cheering and whistling. The trick the petite cowgirl was preparing to do was to throw a wide loop over a rider and his horse as they galloped by. Florence had already thrilled the spectators by roping six running horses with a single twirl of her lariat. She'd also performed the difficult feat of tying a double hitch in slackened rope with two movements of her wrists and demonstrated her agility and endurance jumping from side to side through a loop. There wasn't much doubt she could successfully pull off the next stunt from a prone position, but the audience watched with rapt anticipation.

She spun the rope and tossed it high into the air and it landed around the cowboy and his pinto. She then jumped to her feet and pulled the rope tightly around the two. The fans erupted in applause. She waved at them and bowed appreciatively. For more than twenty years, Florence competed against some of the most accomplished cowgirls in the business for trick and fancy roping championship titles. With few exceptions, she won the contests she entered. It's for that reason she's recognized as "the greatest woman trick and fancy roper of all time."

Florence LaDue is recognized as "the greatest woman trick and fancy roper of all time." PH244_0002, COURTESY OF THE UNIVERSITY OF OREGON.

The talented roper was born Grace Maud Bensel on June 27, 1883, in Chippewa County, Minnesota. Her mother died when she was a little girl, and she was raised by her farmer father. When she was in her teens, she ran away from home and, at some point, signed on with the Cummins' Wild West Indian Congress and changed her name.

While perfecting her roping and riding act at a Chicago show in 1905, she met a cowboy performer from Canada named George "Guy" Weadick. The two fell in love and were married on November 17, 1906. For the first five years of their marriage, Florence and her husband were constantly on the move. They worked with John P. Kirk's Elite Vaudeville Co. and appeared with Will Rogers in his Wild West show. They performed at the Keith-Albee Theater, the Orpheum, and the Pantages and appeared on Broadway in the show *Wyoming Days*. The couple also shared their talent with overseas audiences in Glasgow, London, and Paris.

By mid-1911, Florence was working with the Miller Brothers 101 Ranch Wild West show and squaring off against its star performer, "America's First Cowgirl," Lucille Mulhall. In September 1912, Florence beat out Lucille at the Calgary Stampede Rodeo and was named women's champion in fancy and trick roping. She maintained that title until she retired in 1927.

Once Florence stopped competing, she dedicated herself to helping her husband run the Calgary Exhibition and Stampede Rodeo and the Stampede Guest Ranch, the first guest ranch in Canada.

Florence LaDue passed away on August 9, 1951, in Alberta, Canada. She was sixty-eight years old. ❖

Hazel Hickey Moore

Hundreds of cheering fans flocked to the train depot in Caney, Kansas, on Sunday, October 24, 1920, to welcome the Yankee Robinson Circus to town. When the cast and crew alighted from the multiple cars, the men, women, and children on hand to greet them applauded excitedly. Most of the townspeople followed the performers and workers as they made their way to the location where the circus was to be created. In a flurry of organized chaos, canvas tents were raised; the Big Top was sprawled on the ground and men stood over the seams, lacing pieces together; other men with sledgehammers pounded stakes into the ground at breakneck speed. Teams of men raised enormous poles with combined weight, chanting: "Pull it! Shake it! Break it! Again! Now stake it!" At last, the magnificent translucent tent was in place. Again, the onlookers applauded, in awe of the finely tuned madness.

The following evening, ticket buyers hustled into the tent as tall as the sky and watched in raptured wonder the camels, llamas, zebras, bears, and lions as they were paraded around the arena by trapeze artists, jugglers, clowns, and acrobats dressed in elaborate costumes. A ringmaster hurried to his place in the center of the activity and announced the start of the show. The lights slowly dimmed, and a hush fell over the crowd. Suddenly, a stunning woman on a black horse emerged from somewhere no one noticed and rode out in front of the transfixed patrons. Hazel Hickey, known as the "Prima Donna Equestrienne," led her ride through a series of trots, pirouettes, and canters before serenading the audience with a beautiful rendition of Irving Berlin's song "Blue Skies." She was adorned in an elegant gown of her own making; her hair and eyes shimmered in the spotlights, as did her horse's mane. Hazel urged her ride over to a large box in the middle of the arena, and the animal used his nose to lift the lid. A dozen doves raced out of the box and flew to various points in the rafters. Hazel continued guiding her horse through a myriad of dressage steps while she sang in a high contralto voice. One by one, the doves flew to her and lighted on her head and shoulders and on the back of the horse.[154]

A twenty-two-piece band furnished the music throughout Hazel's performance. At the conclusion of her act, she dismounted her ride and bowed to the audience who applauded appreciatively. Cheers and whistles erupted loudly when Hazel instructed her horse to bow to the crowd. She climbed back on her ride and coaxed the animal to raise his hooves. As the pair exited the arena, Hazel waved to the grateful spectators.[155]

The gifted equestrienne who entertained fans across the country for more than three decades was born Hazel Elizabeth Hickey on June 25, 1902, in Watertown, New York. Her parents, John and Maude, were circus performers. Her father was a horse trainer and trick rider turned canvas superintendent, and her mother was a trapeze artist who excelled at the iron jaw trick. She would be lifted into the air by the trapeze, then she would swing or spin, supported only by a bit clamped between her teeth.[156]

Being raised under the big top, Hazel was exposed to a variety of animals, all of which she enjoyed playing with and helped to train. She attended Catholic school off and on in her early years, but, living on the road, she was unable to establish herself in any one institution. Hazel didn't graduate from high school. Cast members in the circus the Hickeys signed with were responsible for making sure she excelled in the basics of reading, writing, arithmetic, and geography.[157]

Hazel's father instilled a love of horses in his daughter. He was a dressage trainer and developed the gymnastic exercise the horses performed nightly. Hazel expanded on her father's teaching and creat-

You could tell by the way Hazel Elizabeth Hickey Moore dressed when she was growing up that she would be a cowgirl. COURTESY OF LINDA CLARK.

ed dressage demonstrations using multiple horses and riders. She spent her early years in the circus appearing with a troupe of equestrians in group acts executing the tricks she invented.[158]

The respected German horse trainer Max Le Bon spent time teaching Hazel the art of English riding and liberty training. Liberty training is riding bareback and without a bridle. The idea behind it is to build trust and partnership between horse and rider. In her later years, Hazel recalled working with Max as she rode around the circus ring. He used a whip in his training and was so accomplished with it he could tap her on the top of her hands if they weren't correctly placed on the horse's reins. He would also flick her with the whip on top of her knees or the calves if her leg placement wasn't right. Hazel admitted the strict discipline was helpful in becoming an accomplished equestrienne.[159]

Because she was versed in liberty riding, a few of the tricks were performed bareback or resin back. Riders often used resin, a powdery substance that enabled them to maintain a firm grip. Not only did Hazel choregraph a variety of acts, but she also made the costumes the riders wore. Using the small treadle sewing machine she owned, and brightly colored fabric and spangles she purchased, Hazel created outfits and bareback pads adorned with feather plumes, tassels, and sequins.[160]

By the time Hazel turned eighteen, she was featured in an act of her own. She found that the dressage basics, introduced by her father, were an important element in teaching horses in her solo act to jump. Dressage exercises helped the horse feel comfortable with its rider and to trust her. Once she had the horse's trust, she placed a pole on the ground and persuaded the horse to jump over it. She raised the pole up a bit in each training session. Before long, her horse was jumping obstacles more than four feet high.[161]

In 1923, Hazel and her parents were working for the Sells-Floto Circus, the Lockrey Brothers' World-Famous Circus, and John Robinson's Circus. She performed her jumping horse act in all three companies. The posters enticing people to come to the show read, "Miss Hazel Hickey on Count, Highest Jumping Horse in the World!" Hazel had always had confidence in Count's ability. He was one of five horses owned by her father, and the stallion had won several blue ribbons at Southern horse shows. She was so sure of Count's talent she entered the mount in a jumping contest in Louisville, Kentucky, in 1916. Hazel and Count won first place awards in each division of the contest.[162]

By 1924, Hazel was being courted by a number of circus executives to bring her talent to their productions. Her highly sought-after act was the subject of many newspaper articles. "The Walter L. Main Circus introduces to its patrons this year, Miss Hazel Hickey an equestrienne noted for skill as a trainer of high school horses, a rider of unusual skill, graceful pose, hazardous stunts and perfect command at all times of her mounts," the May 24, 1924, edition of the *News Herald* read. "In addition to her remarkable exhibition of menage riding, Miss Hickey with her champion high jumping horse, trained by herself, gives a thrilling display of jumps over the bars."[163]

Walter L. Main sold his circus to the Miller Brothers 101 Ranch Wild West show in late 1924. The Miller Brothers' show had taken a hiatus during World War I, and, at the conclusion of the war, they decided to return to the road with a new lineup of performers. Hazel's work with the 101 Ranch Wild West show was short-lived because the show was struggling financially.[164]

By mid-1925, she was on tour with the Sparks Circus. The massive show traveled by rail, and more than twenty cars were needed to transport performers, animals, and sets. During one of the shows in Iowa in May 1926, Hazel was injured in a bareback riding stunt. According to the May 13, 1926, edition of the *Dubuque Telegraph Herald*, Hazel "misjudged a running leap to the back of the horse." She fell face first off the front of the animal and suffered a fractured jaw when the horse stepped on her. She was immediately transported to the hospital.[165]

The following month, Hazel was back in the ring performing for circus-goers at Bass Park in Bangor, Maine. The *Bangor Daily News* referred to her as the "charming equestrienne who won the admiration of the crowd."[166]

In early 1927, Hazel signed with the Hagenbeck-Wallace Circus, the second-largest circus in America. Promotions for the circus highlighted the many women with the show. "Scores of pretty and comely girls find employment under the mammoth canvas canopy of the Hagenbeck-Wallace Circus, as circus managers have realized for a number of years that nothing attracts the public like an assemblage of beautiful women," an article in the April 28, 1927, edition of the *Evening Standard* read. "Owing to the presentation of a new oriental spectacle, 'The Geisha,' it was necessary to enroll as additional half hundred young lassies for the ballet. These girls were trained for several weeks under the direction of Rex DeRoselli, noted moving picture director.[167]

"The girl performers with the Hagenbeck-Wallace Circus, which is scheduled for two performances here on Friday, are of the healthy, outdoor type. And one will go a long way to find better looking girls than the Marin Sisters, Aerialists; and Hazel Hickey, equestrienne."[168]

Hazel left the Hagenbeck-Wallace Circus a year later and went to work for the Sells-Floto Circus Wild West Show and High School Horse Act. Both circuses were owned by the American Circus Corporation, and the various acts would transfer from one show to the other. The High School Horse Act Hazel starred in consisted of a variety of trick horse performances from high jumping horses to waltzing horses. All riders in the show, including Hazel, wore jodhpurs, full-length trousers that were close-fitting below the knee and made with reinforced patches on the inside of the leg. Hazel made the majority of the jodhpur costumes worn in the act.[169]

Between 1929 and 1930, Hazel lent her talent to the Robbins Bros. Circus. The circus advertised as having the "Earth's Largest Menagerie" and "Bingo, the World's Largest Elephant."

While traveling with the various circuses during the early part of the 1930s, including the Cole Bros. Circus and the Ringling Brothers and Barnum & Bailey Circus, Hazel met a bronc rider named Percy Moore. He competed in rodeos and performed in Wild West shows.[170]

According to Hazel's grandchildren, Percy and Hazel dated briefly before marrying on May 13, 1932, in Kings, New York. The pair continued working and riding for Ringling Brothers after they were wed. Percy participated in rodeos in the cities and towns where the circus was held over. Hazel would take time from her circus act to compete in rodeos at state fairs. She and her horse, Perfect Lady, participated in jumping contests. Perfect Lady was owned by the Moores' friend and part-time employer, Joe Greer. Greer's Society Circus and Wild West Show featured cowboys and cowgirls who rode steers and broncos and were experts at fancy roping, shooting, and jumping horses. Greer believed Hazel was the "finest rider of jumping horses in any arena." Hazel trained Perfect Lady to jump more than seven feet.[171]

The Moores welcomed their first child, Lydia, on March 31, 1933. Their second daughter was born on June 14, 1937. Hazel and Percy were working for the Colonel James Eskew Rodeo and Wild West Show at a New York venue when their little girl made her debut. Her grand entrance into the world made the news. "It is a seven-and-a-half-pound baby girl, who arrived at Percy Moore's tent in Edgerton Park in true frontier fashion at 9:20 P.M. last night," an article in the June 28, 1937, edition of the *Democrat and Chronicle* announced. "There was no physician in attendance upon the mother,

Hazel Hickey, a trick rider in the arena. Her only attendant was Jerry Parker, a western graduate nurse, who travels occasionally with the show.[172]

"The proud parents promptly named their child Percina Rochester. Both mother and daughter are doing well.

"The blessed event heightened excitement occasioned by the arrival of the rodeo in Rochester for its annual two-week stay. Members of the show crowded around the tent which the newly augmented Moore family calls home."[173]

A year after Percina was born, Hazel and Percy left the Eskew show and signed with rodeo performer and Wild West show producer Monte Reger. Reger's show had become popular because of its star, a longhorn steer known as Bobcat Twister. The steer could jump over anything, including a convertible. The Moore family enjoyed its time with Monte Reger's cast, and all was going well until October 6, 1939, when Percy was seriously hurt in the rodeo arena.[174]

"Percy Moore, 34-year-old 'top hand' at the Mississippi-Alabama Fair rodeo, was critically injured when an outlaw horse reared over backward and fell with its full weight on the St. Charles, Iowa, cowboy," the October 7, 1939, edition of the *Clarion Ledger* noted. "Moore had just leaped into the saddle from another horse when Preacher Dunn, described as the worst horse in the rodeo corrals and one used only on special occasions, reared upward and over instead of breaking into a bucking run as usual.[175]

"Moore was unable to free himself from the saddle and the horn struck him in the chest, and the full weight of the seven-year-old horse crushed his legs.

"Rushed to the community hospital, he was believed to have a fractured leg and internal injuries."[176]

When Percy recovered, he and Hazel decided to make a career change. They moved to St. Louis and settled on a ranch near Sylvan Beach that was owned by the Weimeyer family. The couple managed the Weimeyer riding stables on the property and trained horses to be sold to Glenn Randall. Randall trained a number of horses used in such films as *Ben Hur* and the *Black Stallion*. He also trained Roy Rogers' horse Trigger and Gene Autry's horse Champion.[177]

In addition to working with horses, Hazel trained goats. The goats would accompany her to local events where she performed a circus-style act with them. The goats were able to do a variety of tricks and pulled fascinated children in a small cart.[178]

Both Percy and Hazel enjoy teaching their three children how to ride and jump horses. Their daughter Lydia recalled that during the winter months at the ranch Percy would set up a show ring in the barn using bales of hay, and their daughters would ride horses in the ring and help Hazel train the mounts.[179]

In time, Hazel and her family moved to their own home near Fenton, Missouri. Percy went to work for the Absorbent Cotton Company, and Hazel turned her attention to sewing. Excelling at embroidery, one of the first major sewing tasks she accepted after Percy began his job at the Absorbent Cotton Company was making embroidered handkerchiefs for the ladies at the plant.[180]

Both of Hazel's daughters pursued careers as rodeo performers, regaling spectators with their abilities as trick riders and ropers.[181]

Hazel Hickey Moore passed away on July 24, 1977, in Oklahoma City, Oklahoma, at the age of seventy-five.[182] ❧

ROUGH RIDING

Bea Kirnan

B roadside flyers posted around major cities from Amarillo, Texas, to Cheyenne, Wyoming, in 1929 invited rodeo fans to come and see trick roper and bronc rider Bea Kirnan and "gasp with amazement and wonder at her daredevil talent." Audiences were promised to be "thrilled and mesmerized" by Bea's work in the saddle.

BEA KIRNAN ON PINE KNOT TRIANGLE RANCH, (DOUBLEDAY)

Audiences were promised to be "thrilled and mesmerized" by Bea Kirnan's work in the saddle. MEYERS NEG. 4181, B_9161/04181, WYOMING STATE ARCHIVES.

Born on October 9, 1903, in South Dakota, Beatrice Brosseau Kirnan was a champion relayer and Roman rider. Roman riding involved two horses —the rider would stand with each foot on the back of the pair of horses and race around the arena. The balance and leg strength required to perform the act was daunting, and Bea was one of the best Roman riders in the country. She perfected the dangerous trick while working with the Ringling Brothers Circus.

Bronzed and self-reliant, Bea was a rodeo favorite, endowed with beauty that came with perfect physical fitness. From the age of sixteen, she began devoting her every waking hour to competing for riding and roping prizes held between Calgary, Canada, and El Paso, Texas; and between California and Kansas.

Bea held her own against more than a score of young women who made their living bronco riding, trick riding, fancy roping, and even wrestling steers at rodeos. She shared the headlines with such well-known cowgirls as Mabel Strickland, Rene Shelton, Velda Tindell, and Tad Lucas.

While performing in the Miller Brothers 101 Ranch Wild West show in 1915, Bea met an accomplished trick rider named Tommy Kirnan. The two fell in love and married on November 25, 1915, in Chicago, Illinois. Bea and Tommy combined their talents, performing together in rodeos from coast to coast, including such famous venues as Madison Square Garden. The couple was recognized as one of the most famous rodeo duos of the era.

From atop her horse, Rubio, Bea entertained crowds with a variety of difficult tricks, including hanging from her saddle by one heel with her other foot pointing toward high noon while riding full speed across the arena to retrieve a handkerchief off the ground. Bea attributed her successful career as a trick rider to her horse. Rubio had been a gift from a fan who saw her ride in a Wild West show in Latin America. In an article in the August 9, 1919, edition of the *Hutchinson Gazette*, she doted on Rubio. "Do you know, I think Bea thinks more of that pony than she does of her man," the article joked. "Why she was actually seen washing its teeth with a toothbrush."

In July 1922, Bea was injured while performing in a Roman Standing race in Oklahoma. She was riding a pair of spotted ponies when she fell from the steeds as they took a sharp turn. She suffered a broken wrist and was bruised slightly. To make matters worse, someone stole her boots while the doctor was treating her.

Bea retired from roping and riding shortly after her husband passed away in 1937. She found work in a variety of areas including operating a restaurant, designing Western costumes, running a commercial fishing venture, and working in an aircraft plant.

Bea Kirnan was killed in a car accident on December 3, 1960. She was fifty-seven years old. ❧

Lulu Belle Parr

An angry chestnut mare dashed out of the wire enclosure, bucking and twisting. The rider on its back gripped the reins with all her strength. The horse pitched, whirled, and kicked in an attempt to eject the passenger. Lulu Belle Parr, the tenacious cowgirl atop the animal, held on tightly, determined not to be thrown. Despite the bucker's best efforts, Lulu stayed put. The audience watching from the stands surrounding the rodeo arena in Harrisburg, Pennsylvania, erupted with applause. Lulu's strength, skill, and grip of iron in her thighs kept her in place, and the spectators were impressed with her persistence. Rides such as that had earned her the title Wild West show promoters bestowed upon her, "Champion Lady Bucking Horse Rider of the World."[183]

Lady bucking horse champion Lulu Parr. BUFFALO BILL CENTER OF THE WEST, CODY, WYOMING; BUFFALO BILL MUSEUM; MS006-WILLIAM F. CODY COLLECTION; MS6,4075.69.1

Born on November 14, 1876, in Fort Wayne, Indiana, Lulu's love for horses came about at a young age. Her parents, William James Parr and Elizabeth Myers Parr, were reportedly homesteaders who worked the land in a variety of locations from Indiana to Ohio. In 1881, the Parrs moved to Springfield, Illinois, where Lulu and her brother Willie attended Lincoln Elementary School. She preferred to ride her horse to school instead of walk.[184]

When Lulu was in her late teens, she became romantically involved with a farmer named Frank Wheaton who was living in Fernwood, Illinois. She met him during a visit to her Uncle William Sheehan's home in Steubenville, Ohio. The two were to be married until Lulu's father interceded. Wheaton was her third cousin, and her mother objected to the proposed union. When Lulu called off the wedding, Wheaton became furious and brought a lawsuit against her to recover items he had given her in anticipation of their marriage. Among the things Wheaton wanted returned were parlor furniture and a watch. The jury that heard the case determined that Lulu "should keep the presents."[185]

Not long after the court case concluded, Lulu met twenty-two-year-old George Barrett of Jefferson County, Ohio. The pair was married on March 31, 1896. Barrett was a machinist or stationary engineer who maintained motors, boilers, turbines, and ventilators. Lulu and George were married for six years. For most of their marriage, George was abusive and frequently in trouble with the law. She eventually filed for divorce, citing extreme cruelty as the reason.[186]

The one constant in her life ever since childhood was horses. She owned more than five horses when she was married to Barrett and rode as often as she could.[187]

At twenty-seven years old, Lulu decided to pursue a dream she'd been considering for several years. She wanted to use her love of horses and riding in the Wild West shows that traveled the globe. In 1903, Lulu joined Pawnee Bill's Wild West show. As she was just starting out as a rodeo entertainer, she was simply one of the "congress of players" in the program. The advertisement posted in newspapers across the country explained what the cast of Pawnee Bill's production, which now included Lulu, would bring to audiences everywhere. "No country is too far away, none too inaccessible to the energies of the many agents who annually gather this strange ethnological congress together to tour our vast country," the ad in the May 3, 1903, edition of the *Pittsburgh Press* read. "There are hundreds of them, and, coming as they do from many lands and various races, are an instructive feature and a marvel of perfect harmony. Pawnee Bill has been blessed with perspicuity to a lavish degree, and many reckon his show as the largest in America, and over a thousand men and hundreds of horses are actually seen in his grand historic Wild West exhibition."[188]

In a short time, Lulu was featured as one of the top cowgirl acts in Pawnee Bill's show. Her specialty was riding bucking broncos. Lulu was grateful for the chance to work with the show's cast of skilled riders and performers from across the nation. The majority of her castmates were friendly and willing to share their knowledge of horse flesh with other entertainers. However, there were instances when the tension between the cowboys and cowgirls and the Russian Cossacks who rode in the show erupted into a physical altercation. Such was the case in New York in mid-June 1906 when Lulu was injured in one of those disputes.[189]

"There is no feeling of friendship existing between the cowboys and the Cossacks with the Pawnee Bill show at Brighton Beach Park," an article in the June 24, 1906, edition of the *Standard Union* read. "Both are excellent riders, and while the cowboys are not in the least jealous of the Cossacks, they don't like the way they try to run things around the show. They are over-bearing and never lose an opportunity to try to impress the other members of the company with their importance. When riding out of the arena they do so with a careless dash regardless of whom may be standing in the dressing tent waiting to go on.[190]

"During a recent performance, Lulu Parr, one of the cowgirls, was standing in one of the rock concealed entrances waiting to go on as the Cossacks finished their act. Prince Lucca was in the lead of the Cossacks and seeing Miss Parr swung his horse to one side to avoid her. All but the last two of the Cossacks followed him. These deliberately rode her down. The leading horse struck her full in the chest, knocking her down, and the second horse trampled on her, bruising her body and arms, and inflicting an ugly cut on her forehead.[191]

"Captain Jack Lear, of the Rough Riders, saw the occurrence and started after the Cossacks. As he passed the cowboys' quarters, he told them what had happened. Del Champion and Mamie Skeeper, two of the cowgirls, hurried to Miss Parr's assistance, while the cowboys took after the Cossacks. They had probably anticipated the coming of the cowboys and were bunched up with their ugly, heavy Russian swords drawn. They are experts with these nasty weapons, and the cowboys hesitated, but, for a moment. They rode down the Cossacks, knocking them right and left, and, before the latter could reach their horses, the cowboys had them on the ground and beat them unmercifully.[192]

"The Cossacks do not know how to use their fists nor defend themselves in a fistfight. They could only but shout for help as the cowboys rained blow after blow on their faces and bodies. Miss Parr recovered sufficiently to be in at the finish and with her riding whip avenged the wrong the Cossacks had done her."[193]

In June 1908, Lulu was asked to join the Colonel Cummins' Wild West Indian Congress and Rough Riders of the World and travel to England to perform at the New Brighton Tower Gardens. Among those who came to see her ride was King Edward VII. When she returned to the United States, the Wild West show was scheduled to appear in Steubenville, Ohio. Lulu was anxious to let those in the town where she'd lived for so many years see that she'd made good. She planned an elaborate entrance with that goal in mind. She rode her horse from Philadelphia where Colonel Cummins' show was based to Steubenville. The stunt made the front page of newspapers from New Jersey to Montana.[194]

According to the November 30, 1908, edition of the *Salt Lake Herald Republican*, Lulu was to be in Ohio by early December. She would have arrived sooner, but inclement weather detained her. "It is a good six hundred miles from Philadelphia to Steubenville, although the roads are good during the entire distance," the article read. "She [Lulu] has several wagers with friends who have bet that she will abandon the pony before she gets home and finishes the journey by rail." Lulu completed the trip on horseback with never a thought of giving up.[195]

Between 1909 and 1910, Lulu appeared in a variety of shows for the 101 Ranch Wild West program. She was honored to be a part of the Oklahoma-based operation, and, when word reached the press that the "Champion Girl Bronc Buster" would be featured in the show in Brooklyn in May 1910, reporters hurried to interview the cowgirl.[196]

"'The best fun in the world is to ride a bucking horse,'" she assured the correspondent from the *Brooklyn Citizen* newspaper. "'It offers more fun than any pink tea or theatre party or tennis game ever yielded.'" That is the promise given to her sisters in the city by Lulu B. Parr, whose home is the 100,000-acre tract of Oklahoma prairie comprising the famous 101 Ranch. Miss Parr is one of the groups of rollicking girl broncho "'busters'" who will be in this city all next week. She ropes, mounts, and subdues equine outlaws which even the lusty cowboys of the ranch hesitate to approach. She can shoot as quick and straight as the masculine adept and makes a lariat act as if endowed with reason.[197]

"The woman who rides, but who is not intimately familiar with equine species, does not appreciate that she [Lulu] is in as much danger on the back of an impetuous, spirited thoroughbred as in the saddle of a bucker. 'It is impossible ever to thoroughly tame the spirit of the thoroughbred,' Miss Parr shared. 'He may break out at any moment and at any place. Give me the avowedly outlaw horse every time rather than the thoroughbred who is docile one moment and a demand the next.'

"Lulu Parr has as much fun riding a bucker as the audience does watching her ride."[198]

When Lulu received an invitation from Buffalo Bill Cody to join his Wild West show in late 1910, she didn't hesitate. Cody was a legend, and his show was the first of the Wild West programs introduced to the American public. Lulu was associated with a variety of Wild West shows between 1911 and 1913. She rode for the 101 Ranch, Cody, and for Cowboy Billie Burke's show. Cody's show was the most prestigious and well known of all the Wild West shows. One of the first locations she performed with his show was Waterloo, Iowa. The local paper covered the event, focusing on Lulu and how she was related to the famous showman. Much of the article was filled with misinformation that was later used by the Cody show to promote the lady bronc rider.[199]

"The presence in Waterloo yesterday of Wm. F. Cody, 'Buffalo Bill,' was of special interest to Mrs. George H. Myers, 622 Fowler Street, as the noted showman is a relative of hers, having married her mother's cousin," the August 11, 1911, edition of the *Courier* noted. "Her niece, Miss Lulu Parr, also a relative of Mr. Cody, is with the company.[200]

"Miss Parr was entertained at the Myers home for dinner last evening, but Mr. Cody was unable to come as he was busy at the grounds. Mrs. Myers had a good visit with him in his private tent earlier in the day, and the family all attended the performance.[201]

"Miss Parr, who rides the broncos and is the lead in the military tournament in the grand opening, has been with Buffalo Bill for twenty years, having started to travel with him when she was only eight years old. She came of wealthy parentage but, being left an orphan in childhood, accepted the offer of her relative for a place in his show.

"Miss Parr's home was formerly in Canton, Ohio. She is a pretty, young woman, very intelligent and attractive. She is the last of her family as her parents, grandparents, brothers, and sisters are all dead.[202]

"When Mr. Cody, who is now 73 years old, completes this tour, which is his last, he will retire to his ranch near North Platte, Nebraska. At the same time, Miss Parr will retire from public life and will engage in business for herself, her intention being to open a store near her uncle's ranch."[203]

The press agent with the 101 Ranch Wild West show had his own way of promoting Lulu Parr's talent by calling her "one of the most daring and fearless riders with the company." An article that ran in the July 27, 1912, edition of the *Evening Times Republican* and several other newspapers at the same time about Lulu's skill in the saddle, was written by 101 Ranch promoter and cowboy Charles Mulhall.[204]

"Lulu Parr, one of the most daring of the intrepid girls who have won distinction as fearless riders, dauntless hunters, and skillful manipulators of the lariat, is to the manner born, for much of her life has been spent on a ranch, and the range life appeals to her as the only one that is really worthwhile," the *Evening Times Republican* story read. "At first sight, Miss Parr does not suggest the rough, often dangerous life of the range. She is physically made in a mold that suggests daintiness. Paquin gowns and society functions among the ultra-fashionable. As a matter of fact, these things do not appeal to her at all. The restrictions of the evening gown train and the bright lights of the society ball do not allure her in the least. Her greatest pleasure is derived in the saddle, dashing across the prairie on a wild, half-tamed pony, or mingling with the cowboys and doing her part in a thrilling and often dangerously exciting roundup.[205]

"Many times, both on the cattle range and in the 101 Ranch show, Miss Parr has flirted with death and narrowly escaped being a victim of her own daring. Last spring in Philadelphia, when dared to ride a vicious Indian pony which had injured several cowboys, she made the attempt and would have achieved an immediate victory if her saddle girth had not broken and precipitated her to the ground. Although momentarily stunned and painfully injured, she attempted the feat the following day and succeeded in thoroughly taming the 'outlaw.' It was for this victory that Miss Parr received the gold medal which she wears, and which was presented to her by the management of the cowboys as an acknowledgment of her cleverness and intrepidity."[206]

Charles Mulhall, brother to the first "cowgirl" Lucille Mulhall, found Lulu to be everything he noted in the promotional material and more. He fell in love with her, and the two were married in St. Louis, Missouri, on October 25, 1913. Three days after the ceremony, Charles disappeared. Lulu filed for divorce on November 23, 1914, and the grounds for the action was listed as desertion.[207]

Lulu's personal problems did not keep her from continuing with her responsibilities as the world's champion woman bucking horse rider. In January 1914, she traveled with Colonel Cummins' Wild West show to South America. According to the February 21, 1914, edition of *Billboard Magazine*, Lulu made quite an impression on audiences in Buenos Aires, in particular the one-time president of Argentina, Dr. Jose Figueroa Alcorta. The politician showered her with gifts.[208]

When Lulu returned to the United States, she agreed to perform with the Barnum & Bailey Circus. She entertained ticket buyers in New York, Philadelphia, and several other locations throughout the year. During a show in Spokane, Washington, in August 1914, Lulu was thrown from her horse and sustained serious injuries. She wrote one of her relatives about the incident, describing in detail what happened. The letter was written on stationery specifically designed for her by the 101 Ranch Wild West show staff. It featured an image of Lulu on a horse on the top left corner. The right corner included a list of other shows with which she was associated: Pawnee Bill's Wild West, Buffalo Bill's Wild West, and Colonel F. T. Cummins-Brighten Tours.[209]

"My Dear Ralph," her letter dated August 12, 1914, began, "Just a few lines to let you know I am still alive but came near to being sent home to you already for burial. My bucking horse was bucking down the line fine, his head between the fences. I had taken off my big black Mexican hat, and it spooked him. The horse slipped and turned a complete somersault over me. I doubled up in a ball and went under him for he went so quickly. I had no choice to jump—broke my arm—out my eye—doctor took stitches in it—hurt the top of my skull. I am bruised, and there is no feeling on one side of my head. My back cracked as he went over me, and I thought it was broke. [sic] He rolled over, and I rolled away for fear he would fall back on me.[210]

"I jumped up, run out with blood flowing down my face. Doctor sewed my face up, splinted my arm or done it up in boards and splints and bandages, and I am wearing big smoked glasses to protect the sight now and cover up those big, bruised eyes. I am a sight but glad I came out so lucky.

"Inclosed [sic] you a note card. Write me soon. Love to you and Aunt Mag…. Hope the time will soon fly away, and I will see you again soon. I will soon be all right again, and I get my money every week. Well, you never go till God calls you."[211]

Not satisfied with simply being billed as the "Champion Girl Bronco Buster in Wild West Shows," Lulu wanted to make the title official. In May 1915, she decided to register to take part in the World's Champion Bucking Contest at the Frontier Days Rodeo in Prescott, Arizona. She was informed by the rodeo director that there were no contests in the category of lady bucking horse riders, but that she was welcome to compete against the men in that area if she so chose. Lulu must have declined to ride against the men because her name was not listed among those in the event.[212]

Lulu returned to the Wild West shows and worked hard to prove she was worthy of being called a champion in her field. She took part in bronco busting contests in Cheyenne, Wyoming, and earned a number of first prize medals.[213]

There was always a risk of injury when busting broncs, and Lulu had her fair share of injuries riding wild horses. At Pawnee Bill's Pioneer Days in Ohio in May 1915, Lulu suffered a dislocation of the bones of her right knee when a bucking bronco fell on her. She was rendered unconscious for more than thirty minutes, and, when she came to, she returned to the arena, got back into the saddle, and participated in the quadrille on horseback. "The immense crowd cheered her daring," an article in the May 26, 1915, edition of the *Weekly Journal Miner*, reported. "The local physician who attended her after her injury told news reporters that the injury was of such a nature that she should not ride again for two or three weeks, but with her customary nerve and endurance she insisted on mounting her horse and taking part in the program."[214]

Lulu remarried on November 14, 1917. Her third husband was a sailor named Orth B. Barcus. The two were married in Washington, D.C. The time the pair spent apart working their respective jobs took a toll on their marriage, and less than three years later the pair was divorced. Sadly, Lulu had no idea Barcus had filed for divorce.[215]

"Dear Mother, I did not know Orth got a divorce from me," she confessed in a letter home. "I have never received any notification. I am indeed sorry to [*sic*] for I loved Orth, but if he has secured a divorce and don't care to live with me, of course I would not force him to live with me against his will. Nevertheless, I love him as well and ever more now but would like to have notification of the divorce and on what grounds I am sued, and I will never trouble him again with any correspondence. I never got a divorce, and I never will.... Pray for me, mother."[216]

Throughout the course of her career, Lulu distinguished herself not only with her riding style, but also with her manner of dress. From the broad-brimmed sombreros to the multi-laced riding boots, her look was well thought out and unique to her personality. The April 1921 edition of *Billboard Magazine* noted Lulu was one of the "swellest dressed ladies in the Wild West game."[217] An article in the October 20, 1925, edition of the *Florence Morning News* echoed the sentiment and added that few riders had such a stunning wardrobe or could look as good as Miss Parr in the garb. "She is the best dressed of all the cowgirls and girl riders with Miller Brothers 101 Ranch Real Wild West Show."[218]

The same month Lulu was being applauded for being such a well-dressed rodeo star, she married a man who also agreed she was stylish. Tracy Thomas Andrews and Lulu exchanged vows on October 31, 1925, in Newton, Iowa. Andrew was a bull rider with the Cook Brothers Texas Ranch show. The marriage was short-lived.[219]

In the mid-1920s, Lulu performed in a variety of new Wild West shows traversing the United States. In 1926, she rode with the Mammoth Robbins Brothers Big Four-Ring Circus. An article in the July 4, 1926, edition of the *La Crosse Tribune* announced to the residents in La Crosse, Wisconsin, of her coming. "In the Wild West division is Miss Lulu B. Parr of London, England, of Paris, and other European continental places," the report noted. "She is a native of Oklahoma and will appear here and perform her thrilling act. She has appeared in most of the foreign countries as a bronco busting cowgirl rider. Only recently she appeared at the Intercolonial Empire Exposition before the prince of Wales. Later she appeared in the American Rodeo at Paris, France.[220]

"She rides outlaw horses, does anything a man can do astride a cantankerous mustang, and has thrown more wild-eyed mavericks than the oldest 'high-jacking', 'hye-there' bronco buster to be found from the plaza of El Paso to the plains of Moosejaw. She is simply 'it' when it comes to sailing along on the back of a horse. She appears in the Robbins Bros. Circus during the main performance and is an attractive figure at all times."[221]

The following year, Lulu was working for the Hagenbeck-Wallace Circus entertaining audiences in Dover, New Jersey. Among the other women representing the Wild West contingent in late May 1927 were trick riders Julie Rinehart and Hazel Hickey. Lulu was billed as "Ex-Woman Champion Bronc Buster and Bucking Horse Rider."[222]

In 1929, Lulu was still appearing in a number of Wild West shows, including King Brothers Rodeo run by Colonel Jack King. Prominent Westerners appearing under the King banner in addition to Lulu were Vivian Delmore, "Wild Cy" Perkins, Tommy Cropper, Jimmy Carson, and Tom Howard. The riders, both men and women, numbered more than fifty, and twenty-five Sioux Indians were used in the show along with more than a hundred head of stock.[223]

The Robbins Brothers Circus set up its tents in Dodge City, Kansas, on Wednesday, September 18, 1929, and Lulu was listed as one of the stars of the show. An article in the *Dodge City Journal* mentioned how excited residents were to have Lulu visit their town. "She stands without a peer and is the highest salaried rider known to the profession," the newspaper reported.[224]

Throughout the 1930s, Lulu continued to travel the country performing in any Wild West show or circus that invited her. She was in her fifties and still riding unmanageable horses most men wouldn't dare tackle, and she survived bucking tactics without being displaced from the saddle.[225]

The May 17, 1938, edition of the *Gazette and Daily* reported that Lulu had retired to a ranch she owned in Nebraska. The story was only partially correct. She had retired but was living in Riverside, Ohio, with her brother William and sister-in-law Emma. Lulu might have been the "highest salaried rider," but she had little to show for her years as a bronc buster once her career ended. William and Emma were struggling financially as well. The three lived in a small, tar-paper cabin with no water or electricity. Food was scarce, and either Lulu or William would make frequent trips to the gas station across the street from their home to use the restroom and transport buckets of water back with them for cooking and bathing.[226]

Lulu's living conditions were not reflected in her disposition. She always had a kind word for neighbors and was happy to share stories about her days with the Wild West shows. She was seventy-seven when a burglar attempted to break into her feeble home and steal the belongings she had acquired while performing. Lulu leveled a gun at the thief as he entered, and he ran off before a shot was fired.[227]

On January 17, 1955, Lulu was transported to the Miami Valley Hospital in Dayton, Ohio, after neighbors called for help. Lulu was suffering from malnutrition and had had a stroke. Her sister-in-law, who was also ill, was taken to the hospital at the same time. Lulu died sixteen hours after being admitted.[228]

Trunks and cartons of memorabilia collected throughout her time on the rodeo circuit was piled ceiling high in the cabin where Lulu lived. Among those items were costumes, hats, fancy cowgirl belts, and a pair of .45-caliber Colt pistols given to her by Buffalo Bill Cody back in the days she worked for him.[229]

Lulu Parr died on January 17, 1955. Her death certificate listed her occupation as housewife. She was buried in an unmarked grave in the Medway Cemetery in Clark County, Ohio. She was seventy-eight years old when she died.[230] ❧

PART 8

CALF ROPING

Nancy Bragg Witmer

S ome women were just born to the occupation of rodeo performer, trick rider, and trick roper, and Nancy Bragg Witmer was one of those women. Nancy first rode into the rodeo arena to dazzle fans with her talents in 1939. The Kansas native perfected her roping and riding skills as a member of the Tulsa Mounted Troops. The organization trained ambitious young women and men in the art of calf roping and pole bending, a timed event that featured a horse and one mounted rider running a weaving, or serpentine, path around six poles arranged in a line.

While with the Tulsa Mounted Troops (her parents had moved to Oklahoma when Nancy was a child), Nancy caught the eye of well-known equestrian and roping instructor Hank Linton. Linton worked with promising riders to prepare them for an opportunity to work in Wild West shows. Florence Hughes Fenton Randolph, an outstanding trick and bronc rider, was another one of Nancy's instructors. Florence stunt-doubled in Hollywood films for famous actresses in scenes requiring horses jumping over obstacles or ditches. Everything Nancy learned about dazzling fans and moviegoers from atop a horse she learned from the best in the trade.

By the age of sixteen, Nancy was recognized as the nation's premier trick rider. In addition to studying roping and riding, she trained as a dancer and excelled in tap and acrobatic movement. Combining her expertise in dance with her riding aptitude, she invented a maneuver that became her signature stunt in the rodeo ring. Known as "the falling tower," the stunt involved standing in the saddle and doing a backbend while the horse was running at full speed.

Nancy performed "the falling tower" for thousands of enthusiastic fans at rodeo arenas in New York, Boston, Denver, Fort Worth, Tulsa, and Chicago throughout the 1940s. During her time riding in such prestigious rodeos, she appeared with celebrities such as singing cowboys Gene Autry and Roy Rogers, singer-songwriter Bob Wills, and baseball legend Babe Ruth.

In 1950, Nancy began competing in barrel racing, calf roping, and cow-cutting events. She did this while continuing to trick ride. She won several championships, including the coveted GRA World Champion Cutting

Some women were just born to the occupation of rodeo performer, trick rider, and trick roper, and Nancy Bragg Witmer was one of them. SUB. NEG. 25776A, WYOMING STATE ARCHIVES.

Horse title, and was consistently ranked high in rodeo competitions. Nancy's daring exploits in the arena were caught on film in 1954 and aired in the *I Love Lucy* episode titled "Lucy Goes to the Rodeo."

A serious accident during a show at Madison Square Garden in 1956 forced her to retire from the profession at the age of thirty. Four years after putting away her rope and saddle, Nancy married William Bragg, and the couple had three children.

Nancy was inducted into the National Cowgirl Hall of Fame in 1999. She passed away in 2014 at the age of eighty-seven. ❦

Ruth Roach

T he stylish lobby of the Texas Hotel in Fort Worth was a bustle of activity on Saturday, March 11, 1922. Well-dressed patrons were arriving and departing. A string quartet in the corner of the massive entryway serenaded white-haired, prosperous-looking gentlemen and their stocky, bejeweled wives being escorted to their rooms by attentive bellboys. It was dignified confusion with fashionable guests speaking in low, polite tones as they filtered in and out of the restaurant beyond the check-in counter. Conspicuously absent from the scene were cowboy hats, fringed jackets, and cowboy boots. Apart from the enormous painting of a steer roundup hanging over the concierge's gigantic desk to the left of the registration area, there was nothing that would indicate the establishment was Texas based. The refined décor was more like what one would see in New York or Paris.[231]

Suddenly, into this busy, polished setting, cowgirl Ruth Roach appeared riding a spotted pony. She was dressed in white satin knickerbocker pants, wearing a flaming red handkerchief, black cowboy boots, and a huge, white hat. She spurred the animal through the ornate mahogany doors of the establishment, opened for her by a perplexed but accommodating doorman. Society ladies stopped talking, and stockbrokers dropped their newspapers and turned their attention to the horse and rider. Almost simultaneously, the crowd's manner shifted to that of proud Texans, and they shrilled the yell of a cowpuncher, "Yippee! Yee-haw!"[232]

Encouraged by the cries, Ruth urged her mount up and down the length of the lobby several times, standing in the saddle, crossing under the horse's neck, and doing other daring stunts she usually performed at the spring rodeos in town.

Rodeo manager Tom Burnett hurried into the lobby with the announcer for his rodeos, Ben Keith, and led the onlookers in a round of applause. Ruth removed her hat and bowed her head in appreciation. "Ladies and Gentlemen," Ben projected. "May I present Ruth Roach? The most expert horsewoman in the country." The hotel guests cheered loudly. Ruth and her horse performed a few more tricks for the appreciative group. The rubber shoes the horse had been fitted with enabled him to do his job without slipping on the slick tile floor. The guests shouted "Atta-girl" and "Ride 'em" as the pair strutted about.[233]

"Ruth is the undefeated woman rider of the world!" Ben loudly told the noted patrons. "Her grace and gentility are well known throughout the great state of Texas. She has won riding awards in Cheyenne, New York, and London. There is truly none like her."[234]

The inventive publicity stunt conceived by Tom Burnett, and flawlessly executed by Ruth, resulted in a record-breaking crowd at the Southwestern Exposition and Fat Stock Show in Fort Worth. Ruth gave a calf roping demonstration that brought the audience to their feet both nights the rodeo was in town. She was an accomplished rider and fan favorite.[235]

All-around cowgirl champion Ruth Roach had an unmistakable style in riding, roping, and dress. She had a winning smile and topped off every rodeo outfit she wore with a giant bow fixed to the back of her hair. Ruth stood out in a sea of other riders. It wasn't only her look that brought her attention, but also the exciting moves she performed on the back of her horse. In her twenty-four-year-long career with such programs as Buffalo Bill Cody's Wild West show and the 101 Ranch Wild West show, Ruth entertained audiences with daring feats in the saddle that no one could match.

Born in Excelsior Springs, Missouri, on September 17,

Bronco riding was Ruth Roach's favorite event, but she performed and won championship titles in other areas. AUTHOR'S COLLECTION.

1896, Ruth started to ride at her aunt's farm near Springfield when she was three years old. Her parents, John and Anna Scantling, were strict disciplinarians. Her father worked construction, and her mother worked at home raising Ruth and her two younger brothers.[236] Ruth was a rebellious teen. At the age of seventeen, she ran away from home to marry Ivan Montgomery, a student at a local automotive school. Police found the two before they took their vows and escorted them back to their families. Ruth promised to run away again to be with Ivan. She did as she said, and the teenagers found their way back to one another. On September 13, 1912, the two stole a diamond ring from a man in Kansas City and tried to pawn it. The pawnbroker suspected the couple weren't the true owners of the item and phoned the police. Ruth and Ivan were arrested. They told authorities they were married but had no legal documents to support the claim.[237]

Details on what happened between the time Ruth turned eighteen, the day after the arrest, and the summer of 1913 are lacking. What is evident is that she did not stay in Missouri. By June, she was a member of the cast of the Lucky Tull and Yoder Bros. Dog and Pony Show based out of Oklahoma City, Oklahoma. Ruth had hired on as one of the bronc riders for the program and was performing around the country. On June 2, 1913, Ruth suffered a near fatal accident while en route to a show.[238] According to the June 5, 1913, edition of *the Hugo Husonian*, the teenager was asleep on the train that was transporting the troupe to the next town they were to appear. When she woke up, she was confused and didn't know she was on a train. She walked to the side door of the railcar, opened it, and stepped out into the night. The train was moving at a high rate of speed, and when Ruth fell off the railcar she landed hard on her right side. Fellow passengers who witnessed the accident signaled for the engineer to stop the train. The train was then thrown into reverse to return to the spot where Ruth had fallen. Her companions feared she had died, but when they reached the scene, Ruth was sitting near the tracks, patiently waiting for the train. The physicians who examined Ruth could find nothing out of the ordinary outside the injuries to her right shoulder and hip. There were no broken bones.[239]

For more than a year, Ruth rode for Lucky Tull and the Yoder Brothers combined Wild West show. While working in the program, she perfected her ability to ride broncs with and without a saddle. She added trick roping to the act and would entertain audiences by riding around the arena after a pony and tossing a lasso around its neck. A small dog was usually riding on the back of the pony. At some point, she left the Tull and Yoder Brothers' show and joined the popular Miller Brothers 101 Ranch Wild West show. Billed as a trick rider, Ruth rode either standing up on the back of a galloping horse or hanging upside down off the side of the horse while attached to a strap.[240]

While working for the Miller Brothers she met an accomplished cowboy named Jefferson Bryan Roach. Roach was a champion bronc rider. Some historical references note the pair were married on July 15, 1913, and other sources note they were wed in 1919. The two, who made their home in El Dorado, Kansas, were enamored with one another for a time and alternated performing for the 101 Ranch and the Carl Hagenbeck-Wallace Circus.[241]

On March 13, 1917, Ruth made her bronco busting debut at the Southwestern Exposition and Fat Stock Show in Fort Worth. Champion rodeo rider Vera McGinnis was part of the same exhibition. Also in March, Ruth dazzled audiences at the Rio Grande Frontier Days in El Paso with a show of her trick riding skills. It wasn't enough for Ruth to develop her own unique riding style, she created a distinctive look to go with it, too. She wore giant hair bows and boots hand-tooled with hearts. It was easy for rodeo fans to spot Ruth from anywhere in the stands.[242]

Ruth Roach's name was featured prominently on all the advertisements for the 1919 Southwestern Exposition and Fat Stock Show. "Of all the features at the Fat Stock Show and Rodeo none is more thrilling than the riding of cowgirl Ruth Roach," the March 13, 1919, edition of the *Fort Worth Star-Telegram* reported. The picture of Ruth that accompanied the story was of the rider on the bucking bronco known as "Wild Bunch." According to the article, "Wild Bunch is expected to be one of the hardest pitchers she [Ruth] ever attempted to subdue."[243]

In an interview after the stock show, Ruth assured reporters who wanted to know about the dangers of bronc busting that she never got hurt because she was always careful. "I suppose I'm lucky, too, and ought to touch wood," she added. "However, leaving all jokes aside, riding wild horses is my business, and I take up the task like other women tackle sewing, baking bread, etc. I have a system and generally stick to it."[244]

Rodeo fans and journalists alike were charmed by Ruth. An article devoted to the equestrienne that appeared in the April 10, 1919, edition of the *Fort Worth Star-Telegram* reflected the affection many had for her.

"Thrills may be the feature of the sawdust ring, but romance is an attendant," the article began. "Mingling among the crowds of the Fat Stock Show is a small woman clad in the most stylish of costumes; her face radiates happiness as she talks with her comrades. She is Ruth Roach, a girl who made the aspirations of her childhood the facts of her womanhood. This daring rider, beloved by all, found the love of her life in Bryan Roach.... He proved to be the hero of her romance. They eloped. Her ambitions were realized. She became a real show woman.[245]

"...At the Coliseum in Fort Worth, she rode her first bucking horse and won first money. Mrs. Roach has ridden in contests in all parts of the country. She has taken numerous prizes and loves her work with ardor. She declares that someday she will stop and have a home but not until her husband is ready to settle down. They then will stop together. They have ridden together, and they will quit together. Marriage, instead of being the stumbling block in the path to fame, has been the means by which this town-bred cowgirl has achieved her grandest hopes."[246]

Ruth returned to the Fort Worth rodeo in 1920 to compete in the trick riding contest against Kitty Canutt, Florence King, and Dolly Mullins. Ruth also took part in the girl's bronc riding competition at the rodeo and beat Mabel Strickland and Bea Kirnan for the top honor. Kirnan bested Ruth in the trick riding category.[247]

The champion bronc rider participated in every major rodeo from Fort Dodge, Kansas, to Cheyenne, Wyoming. Ruth's husband regularly accompanied her to the shows as he competed in riding and roping events as well. What seemed like a match at the start turned sour by late 1922. The report of their marriage ending made the news in the spring of 1923. "Ruth Roach, beautiful rodeo queen, whose appearance in the arena at the coliseum in recent years, has attracted the admiration of thousands, has entered this time, not the arena but the divorce courts," the April 28, 1923, edition of the *Fort*

Worth Record-Telegram read. "Friday morning through her attorneys, she entered suit in the forty-eighth district court from her husband, Bryan Roach.[248]

"Mrs. Roach, who has thrilled thousands by her daring in the show ring, says she married Roach in Chickasha, Oklahoma, on July 15, 1913, and that they lived together until January 10, 1923. She charges that for the last two years she has been neglected, and she set out in her petition that she was forced to go home alone. 'This proved embarrassing,' she said."[249]

Ruth's personal issues did not keep her from participating in rodeos across the country and winning trick and bronc riding contests several times. She also continued to appear in Wild West shows as their star attraction. She was often billed as "Miss Texas, the Finest Horsewoman that Ever Stepped Across the Texas Border."[250]

In June 1924, she joined a troupe of talented riders, including Rube Roberts, Ambrose "Nowata Slim" Richardson, and Vera McGinnis, in the First International Rodeo. The program, organized by her old friend Tom Burnett, toured Europe, and Ruth performed for kings and queens of a handful of countries. While performing overseas, she fell in love with fellow rider and world champion cowboy Ambrose "Nowata Slim" Richardson. According to the January 2, 1927, edition of the *Times Union*, the two wed in late 1924. They spent rodeo season on the road and in the winter months at their ranch in Lenapah, Oklahoma.[251]

By May 1925, Ruth was back in the states competing in bucking bronco contests and winning prizes at the Cisco Rodeo finals in Cisco, Texas, and the Pendleton Roundup in Pendleton, Oregon. An article in the June 4, 1925, edition of the *Indiana Weekly Messenger* proved how popular Ruth continued to be. "Cowgirls do exist outside the pages of fiction and away from the motion picture camera," the story began. "They ride and rope with the best of the boys in chaps and Stetsons, and, in fact, they exceed in skill and daring some of the male busters of the range. Many of these women riders will participate in the Chicago roundup and world's championship rodeo which will be held in Grand Park Stadium beginning August 15. Among the most famous of these is Ruth Roach of Fort Worth, Texas. Her daring as a rider has become proverbial as a result of dashing exhibitions of skill in the saddle at previous rodeos."[252]

At Frontier Days in Cheyenne, Wyoming, in July 1925, Ruth thrilled the crowd watching the cowgirls bucking contest. She rode a horse named Paleface that had a reputation for being "the most vicious bucker that had crossed the pike." First, Paleface dived nose down into the ground, then rolled over, smashed Ruth against the fence, tore the fence away, reared up on his hind legs, nosedived again and tore off some more fence, and then started in regulation bucking style. Ruth rode Paleface until the horse gave up. Her pluckiness drew cheers from the many fans watching the event.[253]

Ruth remained one of the country's favorite rodeo performers through-out the latter part of the 1920s and into the 1930s. During that time, she and Nowata Slim divorced. She then married and divorced rodeo director and steer wrestler Fred Alvord. Fred and Ruth were involved in a domestic violence dispute that resulted in Ruth being barred from competing in any rodeos in El Paso, Texas. The newspaper account of the event noted that during an argument the pair were having in a moving car, Fred opened the door and Ruth kicked him out. Before evicting him from the vehicle, she blackened his eye and tore his shirt off.[254]

"We went to Juarez for a party, and when we came back Ruth wanted to fight," Fred told police. I tried to get out of the car, but she tore my clothes off and beat me up before I could fall out." Ruth claimed it was Fred that got rough and that she was trying to 'sober him up.'"[255]

March 1930 found Ruth as a repeat contestant in the Southwestern Exposition and Fat Stock Show. She entered the bronc and trick and fancy riding competitions as an ex-champion in each event. She hoped the good showings she'd had in rodeos in New York, Chicago, Calgary, and Cheyenne in the past year would help her win in both events. Sadly, she was thrown from a bronc early and couldn't perform as she usually did.[256]

From 1931 to 1933, Ruth took part in Wild West shows and rode in special benefit rodeos. She was in her late thirties and struggled to bounce back after getting thrown. While participating in a charity rodeo at Madison Square Garden in 1933, she broke her ankle when she was tossed off a bucking horse. A year later, she broke her wrist in a bronc busting exhibit in Fort Worth. The injuries helped with her decision to retire from the sport.[257]

Ruth might have removed herself from rodeo competitions, but that didn't mean she was out of the limelight. She appeared in parades, lent her image for advertisements for upcoming rodeos, and even worked in silent films alongside Tom Mix.[258]

In late February 1939, Ruth made another trip down the aisle. This time, she married a cattle rancher named Richard Salmon. The two lived a quiet life on his ranch near Nocona, Texas.[259]

Ruth Roach Salmon died on June 25, 1986, in Fort Worth, Texas, at the age of ninety-two. She was laid to rest at the Nocona Cemetery, near the home she shared with her husband.[260] ❦

PART 9

RELAY RACING

Donna Card

Professional bronc rider Kitty Canutt grabbed a stick of wood lying next to a horse stall at the rodeo grounds in Spokane, Washington, and smacked champion relay racer Donna Card in the mouth with it. The incident occurred in early September 1918 and was the start of a feud between the cowgirls that would continue until their passings.

Kitty Canutt didn't take losing relay races well. She once thought Donna Card had cheated her out of a win and hit her in the head with a chunk of wood. PH244_0008, COURTESY OF THE UNIVERSITY OF OREGON.

Kitty, wife of famed Hollywood movie stuntman Yakima Canutt, was upset with Donna over the way she behaved in the women's relay race at the Spokane Rodeo. She claimed Donna fouled her in the third lap by crowding her into the fence. She complained to the judges, and, after investigating the charge, they determined Donna had run a clean race. Kitty was furious over the ruling and confronted Donna about the perceived indiscretion. Kitty was disqualified from riding in any other events at the rodeo and was fined $25 for her violent outburst. Donna went on to win the trophy as top relay racer.

Missoula, Montana–born Donna Card was a horseback riding phenom-enon. She was an expert trick roper and fancy rider who won numerous championships, but her expertise was the women's relay. Often associated with the Drumheller Company, a respected ranching firm that raised thoroughbred horses used in relay races, Donna was considered by rodeo enthusiasts to be one of the best women riders in the field.

The relay race required riders to make three laps around the track, changing horses at the end of the first and second laps. It was compulsory for riders to touch the ground with both feet when making horse changes. Early on, the relay race was considered a man's game because of the danger and physical effort necessary in changing mounts. Donna was one of a few who proved women could become as good in the ranch sport as the men.

Donna frequently competed against accomplished relay racers Vera McGinnis and Mary Harsh. The women's relay was considered by most rodeo attendees as the most spectacular of the events. Vera and Donna generally finished first and second in the contest, with Donna beating Vera for the top spot most of the time.

In 1918, Donna's big win at the Spokane Rodeo made headlines. "Among the most interesting races of the day was the women's relay, in which three strings were entered," an article in the September 3, 1918, edition of the *Spokesman Review* read. "Miss Donna Card, clad in blue and white silk, was the winner, negotiating the two miles in three minutes forty-seven seconds."

Donna defeated the world's champion relay racer, Mabel Strickland, at the Spokane fair in September 1922. She took a commanding lead in the first lap and held it throughout the race. She outrode both Mable and Kitty Canutt.

In addition to being recognized

Missoula, Montana-born Donna Card was a horseback riding phenomenon. COURTESY OF COWGIRL MAGAZINE.

for her efforts in relay racing, Donna was also a fashion trendsetter. The blue satin riding skirt, white jersey, and patent leather slippers worn at the Yankee Stadium Rodeo in New York in 1923 was duplicated by clothing designers in attendance and sold to the public. ✦

Bertha Kaepernik Blanchett

Fashionably dressed bronc rider Bertha Kaepernik picked herself up from the dust and mud of the rodeo arena in Cheyenne, Wyoming, in August 1904, and wiped the dirt out of her eyes. She had just been thrown from a big gray horse, a bucker of the worst type. "Why of course I'm going to ride him again," she told the rodeo officials. The charming and resilient cowgirl from Sterling, Colorado, was determined to show the crowd that the hard fall she had just received was merely a slight incident in the life of a woman who wanted to make a name for herself busting outlaw horses.

The big gray was brought back after a long chase down the arena, and Bertha once more swung into the saddle. Spurs were sunk, and the quirt was brought down on the animal's flanks; however, he was tired of the routine and merely stampeded, much to the disgust of the daring rider.

Urging her horse back to the judge's stand, Bertha called for another horse. A little roan containing the combined elevating power of a volcano and a charge of dynamite was brought out and duly saddled after a hard fight in which the animal tried to kill the horse wrangler by striking the man down with iron-shod hooves. The roan's cantankerous attitude didn't seem to phase Bertha. She was ready for whatever was to come.

Grasping the saddle horn with one hand and deftly inserting one foot in the stirrup and then swinging into the saddle with a nicety that left her well balanced for any jump the horse might make, Bertha was away on her rough voyage. The roan proved to be a better bucker than the big gray that had thrown her. He pitched and flipped and changed ends, but Bertha was in the saddle to stay. She rode upright until the horse fairly wore himself out.

Born in Cleveland, Ohio, in 1883, Bertha Kaepernik made history in 1904 by becoming the first woman to ride a bucking horse at Cheyenne Frontier Days. She would go on to win the bucking championship at the Pendleton Roundup in Oregon in 1911, 1912, and 1914.

Not only was Bertha an accomplished bronco buster, but she also established the world's record for the Roman race, making a quarter mile in eight seconds at Pendleton. She also set a record for a female Roman rider at the Washington rodeo in Walla Walla.

In 1909 she married Dell Blanchett, a trick rider for the Bison Moving Picture Company. He was killed in action during World War I.

In addition to competing in rodeos, she was a stuntwoman working on some of the first Western films that starred Tom Mix and Hoot Gibson. She traveled extensively across the United States and Europe while working for Pawnee Bill's Wild West show and the 101 Ranch Wild West show. When her career in rodeos and motion pictures ended, she became a guide at Yosemite National Park. She died at the age of ninety-five on July 3, 1979. ✦

Bertha Blanchett honed her riding skills performing with the Miller Brothers 101 Ranch Wild West show. PH244-0230
COURTESY OF THE UNIVERSITY OF OREGON.

Claire Thompson

When the Miller Brothers 101 Ranch Wild West show paraded down one of the main thoroughfares in Kansas City, Missouri, on April 27, 1925, leading the way was an attractive twenty-three-year-old cowgirl named Claire Belcher, dressed in a colorful fringed outfit and riding atop a white stallion. The talented rodeo performer hadn't been with the Wild West program long and was beaming with pride to be at the front of the march announcing that the show had come to town. Behind her were cowboys on horseback, stagecoaches, wagons pulled by elephants, and a band perched atop a massive truck serenading cheering fans as the cavalcade passed.[261]

The Miller Brothers' show originated in Oklahoma on their 110,000-acre ranch near Ponca City. The show routinely appeared in big towns such as New York, Cleveland, and Kansas City. Among the well-known people who had traveled to see the extravaganza over the years were Presidents Warren G. Harding and Theodore Roosevelt, newspaper mogul William Randolph Hearst, and the famous scout Buffalo Bill Cody. Claire was thrilled to have been asked to sign on with a show that boasted such exceptional female riders in its past as Lucille Mulhall and Lulu Belle Parr. She was dedicated to being as good an equestrienne as they were and to excelling in the rodeo profession.[262]

Born Gladys Rogers Emmons on February 9, 1902, in Mansfield, Massachusetts, the young woman was more interested in gaining and keeping her mother Florence's attention than riding. In fact, she was nearly twenty years old when she first became interested in horses. Florence divorced Gladys' father, Henry Emmons, when the child was five years old and moved to Texas with her daughters. The couple had a second child named Florence Frances. Not long after arriving in the Southwest, Florence had a change of heart and returned to the East Coast with Gladys in tow. After explaining to her parents, David E. Harding and Frances Rogers Harding, why she could no longer care for the little girl, she hurried back to Texas, leaving Gladys behind. Gladys' grandparents were devoted to raising her and making sure she had a proper education. The Hardings were wealthy landowners whose money had been made in the manufacturing business. In addition to being a business tycoon, Harding was a banker and involved in politics. They resided on an estate called Rockrimmon. Gladys would lack for nothing except her mother's affection.[263]

When Florence left Massachusetts without her child in 1905, she married a rancher from San Antonio, Texas, named Colonel William Furlong. Their divorce in the fall of 1912 made front-page news with Florence accusing Furlong of being cruel and abusive and Furlong accusing Florence of being a pathological liar. David Harding passed away three years prior to the Furlongs' divorce being finalized. Harding left everything to his wife and daughters. Florence traveled back and forth between Rockrimmon and the San Antonio ranch where she trained horses. Neither Gladys nor her sister were a priority to their mother.[264]

Gladys' aunt, Florence's sister Mabel Barnes, was a major influence in her life. Not only was she a gifted pianist who shared her love of music with her niece, but she was also an accomplished English-style horseback rider. Mabel taught Gladys how to ride and found the young woman had a distinctive flair for the sport. After Gladys graduated from high school, she attended LaSalle Junior College where she studied piano. At the urging of her Aunt Mabel, she went on to attend the New England Conservatory of Music in Boston. When Gladys completed her studies, she returned to Rockrimmon and to riding. She became proficient in dressage and performed in exhibitions and competitions throughout the state.[265]

In the spring of 1920, Gladys married a former soldier named Sumner B. Kirby from Norfolk, Massachusetts. Kirby had fought in World War I and the pair met through a mutual friend. The couple had a daughter the following year, but the child died from meningitis less than a month after she was born. Gladys sunk into a deep depression, unable to carry on for a short while. Her marriage did not survive the tremendous loss. Sumner and Gladys were divorced by the end of 1922.[266]

Friends concerned about Gladys' emotional state invited her to attend a rodeo in the town of North Adams, Massachusetts. She reluctantly agreed to go along, and it was there she met a bulldogger named Bob Belcher. The steer wrestler and the lady dressage rider shared their knowledge of horseflesh with one another and quickly bonded. The pair were married after a brief courtship and turned their attention to life on the rodeo circuit. Gladys was fascinated with bulldogging, and Bob was happy to teach his bride all he knew about the sport. She was fearless and enjoyed jumping off the back of her ride, grabbing hold of the steer's horns, and bringing it to the ground. When the Belchers signed with the Miller Brothers 101 Wild West show in 1925, both listed bulldogging as an area in which they could perform.[267]

When Gladys rode her horse into the rodeo arena in Kansas City, Missouri, she had a new name. Billed as Claire Belcher, she was the Miller Brothers' only female bulldogger. Newspaper articles not only celebrated

Claire's "bravery and strength," but also made note of her beauty. A story in the April 26, 1925, edition of the *Sedalia Democrat* pointed out that the 101 Ranch Wild West show had some of the most striking women in the profession in their cast.[268]

"Are the girls with Miller Brothers' Wild West any different from the girls in your hometown or mine?" the *Sedalia Democrat* article began. "Not a bit, except that the 101 young women are daring, expert riders, instead of secretaries, stenographers, teachers, or sales ladies. There are many girls of prominent families among the hosts of beauties with the biggest of all Wild West shows.[269]

"When 101 comes to town, you'll be surprised at the attractiveness of the femininity, and you will wonder if Flo Ziegfield did the picking when the world's largest and most picturesque street parade swings by. But you will conclude, when you see Mamie Frances, Rena Hafley, Mildred Hinkle, and Claire Belcher and scores of others equally as pretty members, that the Follies chorus has gone into the cowgirl racket."[270]

After performing for more than a month at various locations throughout Missouri, Claire and the troupe traveled to Massachusetts. She was thrilled to be in her home state and hoped her family would be able to see her work. Not only had she learned to wrestle steers, but she was also a gifted trick roper and rider. Just as she had in Kansas City, Claire led the parade of performers into Boston on May 31, 1925.[271]

"Several thousand small boys and girls went home last night with wonderful tales for the stay-at-homes of scores and scores of real Indians, resplendent in pain and feathers, of buffaloes, broad-hatted cowboys, swift, sleek horses, and lurching ox teams," an article in the June 1, 1925, edition of the *Boston Globe* read. "And the youngsters weren't the only ones who watched the arrival and setting up of the Miller Brothers' 101 Ranch Wild West show. Thousands of grownups were there, too, and seemed equally interested.[272]

"The show, which is claimed to be the largest Wild West show ever assembled, pulled into the Boats and Maine yards at Front Street about 7 o'clock yesterday morning. Soon afterward the vanguard of orange and blue wagons had reached the lot where the show will take place. With amazing celerity, the cook tent went up, and before noon most of the big canvas city had been erected."[273]

When Claire wasn't performing in the Miller Brothers' show, she and Bob were competing for titles at various rodeos. In the summer of 1926, the pair participated in events in Oregon, Nebraska, Wyoming, and Kansas. Bob took second place at the rodeo in Falls City, Nebraska, in mid-July 1926. Claire didn't take home any prize, but newspaper reports referred to her as "one of the best trick and fancy riders in the game."[274]

By late fall 1926, Claire was listed in the 101 Ranch Wild West show's program as the "World's Champion Cowgirl Steer Wrestler." She dazzled audiences at the Texas Cotton Palace in Waco from November 1 to November 4. "In this suicidal stunt, which is called a sport," a story about Claire in the *Waco News Tribune* read, "the cowboy is mounted on a fleet footed cow pony, chases a wild longhorn, and when he has brought his mount within leaping distance of the steer, he leaps from the saddle, grasping the bovine by the horns, when a hand to horn battle ensues.[275]

"The wild steer, which defies all efforts at subjugation, tries with might and main to gore the life out of the wrestler, while the wrestler by the application of scientific means, is able to overcome the great handicap of weight and brute animal strength, and throws the steer flat upon its side.[276]

"It is a wild battle, a desperate stunt, requiring lots of grit and nerve, and there must be science also, or the wrestler is apt to lose his life. Imagine, then a strip of a girl weighing but 138 pounds leaping from a flying cow pony and grasping an enraged wild Longhorn steer by its ungloved horns and wrestling it to earth in true Western fashion, and you have a picture of one of the many thrills that will be presented during the rodeo at the Cotton Palace."[277]

Claire set a record at the Cotton Palace Rodeo when she threw a steer in eight-and-four-fifths seconds. A mighty shout went up from the crowd in the grandstand when her time was announced. Rodeo patrons fascinated by the notion of a woman bulldogger clamored for more information about Claire. The *Brooklyn Daily Eagle* obliged the curious with an article about the "charming debutante" that appeared in the November 13, 1927, edition of the publication.[278]

"My weight is against me," Claire noted in the *Brooklyn Daily Eagle* story. "The girl who was my real rival for the championship is much bigger than I. But that isn't what matters, I don't think. I guess it is skill—maybe pep—that counts." If you ever got one good, close-up look at Claire Belcher you would understand exactly what she meant by having weight against her. She was positively so thin that she did not look strong enough to do any riding, let alone steer dogging and bronc riding. It is not strength that counts, she pointed out. It's skill and not being scared.[279]

"Claire Belcher figures things out and analyzes them a little differently than most of the girls who ride in the rodeos. She learned a good deal about analysis and introspection while she was at college. And she gets the best of a good many ponies because she uses her head while she is riding them.[280]

"Of all the unusual professions that the girls of her class at college are engaged in, Claire Belcher's job is probably the most unusual. She is a cowgirl who does all kinds of daredevil work because she enjoys doing it. For years she went to schools in the East, first to a famous finishing school, and then to college. Her parents lived out West, and her mother had a thousand-acre ranch. But everyone supposed that Claire would lose a little interest in horse-flesh after she got away from the Panhandle, where a good pony is still valued considerably higher than the best automobile.[281]

"…It is only a few months now since she has been riding in the rodeos, and in that short time she has piled up a few championships to her credit. 'Is it dangerous?' smiles Claire. 'Well, I guess you might call it that. A little while ago I was racing in a relay and my pony fell with me. I was in the lead and there were four girls coming on in back. Most of the ponies just walked right over me and mashed me up. The newspapers back home printed articles that said I was about dying.[282]

"'I have had quite a few accidents,' she admits. 'Last month I broke my hand and last week one of my ribs was broken. The hand, though, bothers me more than the rib.

"'But I was lucky because you always ride a bronc with your left hand, and when you throw a steer you use your left hand and your right shoulder. So, I really got a lucky break!

"'Of course, I don't think the business is any more dangerous than any other. I was visiting my grandmother a few weeks ago, and I heard of more accidents than I had for a long time. One man fell against some electric wires and was electrocuted, another was run down by an auto and something happened to two other people. The main way we keep safe while we are riding broncs is to fall clear of the ponies and to keep our heads while we are falling and after we've hit the dust.[283]

"'Now take bulldogging. It really isn't dangerous. The steer does not like being thrown, but if he acts too mean you turn him free and then get out of his way.

"'...It's all pretty hard work, but I wouldn't want to do anything else.'"[284]

Claire Belcher frequently participated in other events at rodeos besides bulldogging. She also entered bronc and trick riding and roping contests. At rodeos in Kirksville, Missouri, and Aurora, Illinois, in the late 1920s, she placed first and second in the lady bronc riding and trick roping events.[285] The highly educated cowgirl expected to sustain injuries at the various exhibitions in which she took part. At a rodeo in Chicago in August 1927, Claire was thrown from her horse while making a turn in the women's relay race. The animal had stumbled and fallen, tossing Claire over its head and onto the ground. Before she could get to her feet, she was trampled by another horse.[286]

The field of lady bulldogging wasn't a crowded one. Besides Claire, the other popular woman steer wrestler was Fox Hastings. The pair often competed against one another.[287] The press played up the professional rivalry between the two and reported every occasion Claire and Fox met in the rodeo arena. The women were scheduled to square off against each other in October 1927 at Madison Square Garden to determine the best steer wrestler. The winner would receive $5,000. The *Messenger Inquirer* newspaper mentioned the upcoming showdown in the October 20, 1927, edition of the publication. Claire promised to not only beat her own bulldogging record but also "take the championship crown away from Fox."[288]

Claire made good on her promise, winning the title of "Champion Girl Steer Dogger of the World" at the New York rodeo.[289]

The animosity between Claire and Fox spilled over onto their spouses. Shortly after Claire outrode Fox at Madison Square Garden, Bob Belcher and Michael Hastings got into a physical altercation over the contest. Belcher charged Hastings with disorderly conduct, and the latter was fined $5. Those who witnessed the exchange told law enforcement officials the battle between the two was the result of Hastings being jealous that Belcher's wife was a "better horsewoman."[290]

Claire's fame continued to grow throughout 1928. She was featured on the cover of magazines and was the headline act at Wild West shows across the country and abroad. In addition to being a member of the cast of performers with the 101 Ranch Wild West show, Claire was a part of California Frank Hafley's Wild West Show and Rodeo and traveled to Cuba and Canada to entertain audiences.[291]

Just when Claire's popularity was at its zenith, her relationship with Bob Belcher plummeted. On December 16, 1928, Claire filed for divorce. Five months after she and Bob went their separate ways, Claire was injured trying to throw a steer at a rodeo in Memphis, Tennessee. She was taken to the hospital where she was treated for a concussion and severe body bruises. She recovered quickly and went on to participate in rodeos and perform in Western shows from Nebraska to New Mexico. Along the way, she met a bulldogger named Jack "Red" Thompson. The two were married in the fall of 1929. Red was an accomplished steer wrestler with numerous championship titles to his credit. Like Claire, Red was also a trick roper.[292]

From 1930 to 1934, the couple toured the United States and Canada, showing off their bulldogging skills, racing in relays, and demonstrating their trick roping and riding talents everywhere they went. In 1934, Claire and Red traveled to England with Tex Austin's Wild West Show and entertained rodeo fans at the White City Stadium in London. While the Thompsons were en route to Europe, they made the acquaintance of a roping horse named Hog Eyes. The bay experienced some difficulties onboard the ship to England. He received a deep wound from a protruding piece of wood that struck him in the neck, which later became infected. Red and the horse's owner tended to the animal's injury; when the owner was busy riding in the rodeo, Red took over full-time care of Hog Eyes.[293]

Claire and Red stayed with the horse around the clock until the wound healed. The Thompsons became attached to the horse, particularly Red.

Without her husband knowing, Claire approached Hog Eye's owner and asked if he would consider selling her the animal. The man agreed. Red was moved to tears by Claire's gift. Back in the United States, Hog Eyes and Red performed in rodeos everywhere, winning numerous steer wrestling contests. The bond between them continued to grow, and Claire was pleased to see how happy her husband was with the horse.[294]

Claire's career flourished in the 1930s. She took home numerous prizes for bulldogging and bronc riding. Claire had a black pony named Hobo that helped her win top awards. Hobo was used exclusively for trick riding. Her friends on the rodeo circuit often remarked how pampered the horse was and commented on the numerous products Claire used to always keep him looking his best. She kept a bottle of curling fluid in his stall at all times and daily gave the hair on his hips a checkerboard coiffure before each performance.[295]

Claire Belcher Thompson was an international star and a dynamic competitor and performer. COURTESY OF THE NATIONAL COWGIRL MUSEUM AND HALL OF FAME.

Beginning in the fall of 1936, a series of unfortunate events altered the course of rodeo life for the Thompsons forever. Claire was busting broncs at a competition at Madison Square Garden on October 20, 1936, when the horse she was riding injured her. She had successfully completed a ride atop a cantankerous animal named Firefly. One of the pickup men was transferring Claire from Firefly to his horse when Firefly lashed out with his hind feet and kicked her in the leg.

Claire was quickly transported to a hospital where she had to undergo surgery to save the limb. Further operations were required to fully restore the broken bones. It took months for Claire to completely recover.[296]

In 1938, it was Red's turn to deal with health issues. He had been gored by a steer at a rodeo in Nebraska in August 1936, and surgery was required to repair puncture wounds to his intestine. Two years later, the problems from the injury flared and forced Red to retire from riding.[297]

After winning the cowgirl's bronc riding contest in Fort Worth in October 1939, Claire decided to limit the number of rodeos and shows in which she appeared to care for Red full-time. She supplemented their income by writing for the rodeo magazine *Hoof and Horns*. Her regular column, "Cowgirl's Comments," introduced readers to some of the rodeo's top male and female performers. In 1941, Claire joined the cast of the Rodeo Bar C Ranch program in Fort Worth. She worked alongside top cowgirls Bea Kirnan and Tad Lucas. She took part in the first all-cowgirl rodeo in Bonham, Texas, in the summer of 1942.[298]

In February 1946, the international rodeo star opened the doors to a riding school she founded called the Western Riding Academy. Classes were held at the Dorman Ranch outside Fort Worth. The slogan that attracted students to Claire's school was "Learn to ride as the cowboys ride." The creation of the academy was born out of Claire's love for riding and because Red's hospital bills were insurmountable; she needed funds to keep the creditors at bay. He needed continual medical attention for help with his stomach. Rodeo friends of the Thompsons gave her ponies, saddles, and horses for her students.[299]

When Claire wasn't teaching students how to ride like a cowboy, she was at home in Fort Worth with Red. Hog Eyes never ceased to be an important part of the bulldogger's life. Claire made sure Red was with the horse as often as possible. Many offers were made to buy Hog Eyes, but Claire refused to sell him. Red's condition continued to deteriorate, and, by 1945, he had gone blind. His horse remained one of the key sources of comfort to him. When he was hospitalized in May 1950 and it was clear Red wasn't going to live much longer, he told Claire he wanted to be with Hog Eyes one last time. Claire managed to sneak the horse into the hospital through a freight elevator and bring the animal to her husband's bedside. Red died on May 9, 1950.[300]

It took some time for Claire to move on after Red's death. She eventually returned to competition and to working as a columnist for another magazine, writing about the industry. She opened another horseback riding school in 1953 in Bandera, Texas. Somewhere during her travels to various stables in the Fort Worth area searching for horses to purchase for her school, she met Frank Lohre. Frank was a retired rodeo bronc rider working as the manager of Cobb Park Stables. The two married and became co-managers of the facility.[301]

The Lohres decided to leave Texas in 1959. Frank opened a mobile horseshoe shop in Jacksonville, Florida. The business proved to be hugely successful.[302]

Claire Belcher Thompson Lohre died on April 11, 1971, at the age of sixty-nine at her home in Lake City, Florida. She was laid to rest beside her Aunt Mabel in Mansfield, Massachusetts, at the Spring Brook Cemetery. The tenacious bulldogger was inducted into the Rodeo Hall of Fame at the National Cowboy and Western Heritage Museum in Oklahoma City, Oklahoma, in 2008.[303] ◆

PART 10

HORSE DIVING

Mamie Francis

Cowgirl Mamie Francis sat atop her horse, Babe, waiting for the director of California Frank Hafley's Wild West show to let her know when the program began. Mamie and Babe were perched on a wooden platform thirty feet in the air over Coney Island, New York, looking down at the audience in the grandstands. Directly below the platform was a forty-foot tank filled to overflowing with water. It was the summer of 1908.

Mamie gently urged Babe to the edge of the platform. Both stood like a beautiful statue surveying the landscape before them. After receiving the signal, Mamie coaxed Babe forward. The horse pushed away from the boards and lunged outward into space. Moments later, rider and horse entered the water in the tank with a giant splash. When they came to the surface, the audience erupted in applause. Mamie patted Babe's neck as the horse carried her up the ramp and out of the tank.

Born in Nora, Illinois, on September 8, 1885, to Charles and Anna Ghent, and given the name Elba Mae, Mamie was an accomplished equestrienne by the time she turned sixteen. Her parents moved from Illinois to Wisconsin when she was a baby. Her mother worked for a farmer who owned several horses, and it was there she learned how to ride and use a gun to hunt. When Pawnee Bill's Wild West show stopped in Kenosha, Wisconsin, for a two-night performance, Mamie was in the audience to take in the excitement. Before the show left town, she had signed on to be one of the entertainers.

As Mamie excelled at riding and shooting, that's what Pawnee Bill had her do in the show. In time, she would be billed the greatest horseback and rifle shot in the world. Mamie met her first husband, trick rider Herbert Skepper, shortly after joining the show. The pair was married on July 7, 1901.

By 1905, Mamie had left the Pawnee Bill's Wild West show and divorced Skepper. Charles Francis Hafley and his wife, trick shooter Lillian Smith, were familiar with Mamie's talents and sought her out to join Hafley's Wild West show. She happily agreed to be a part of the troupe. During her time with the experienced group, Mamie perfected her own sharpshooting routine, tried her hand at bronc riding, and even mastered a few rope tricks.

Known as the "Diving Equestrian," Mamie Francis and her horse made over six hundred jumps between 1907 and 1914.
COURTESY OF COWGIRL MAGAZINE.

In late 1907, she added horse diving to her repertoire. Known as the "Diving Equestrienne," she and Babe made over six hundred jumps between 1907 and 1914.

When Mamie stopped horse diving, she turned her attention solely to sharpshooting, trick riding, and training horses to compete in dressage* events. Mamie married Charles Hafley in November 1909, a year after he and Lillian Smith divorced. The two managed the Wild West show for thirty-one years.

Mamie Francis Hafley died on February 15, 1950. She was sixty-four years old.

The National Cowgirl Museum and Hall of Fame honored Mamie for her equestrienne skills in 1981. ❦

---

*The art of riding and training a horse in a manner
that develops obedience, flexibility, and balance.*

Adele Von Ohl

The mesmerized onlookers lining the streets in Denver, Colorado, in 1913 were treated to a grand Wild West show entourage. The crowd cheered as showman Buffalo Bill Cody proudly led his cast and crew down the thoroughfare toward the parade field where they would be performing. The lengthy caravan consisted of 181 horses, eighteen buffalo, elk, donkeys, the Deadwood stagecoach, high-riding cowboys, brave Indian warriors, and a select group of women known as Cody's "American Amazons."

The ladies who made up the American Amazon act possessed a variety of talents, all of which were guaranteed to "thrill and entertain" audiences. Among the popular Amazons was the charming Goldie Griffith. Griffith was a gifted horsewoman with a flamboyant reputation. She was a steer wrestler as well as a rider. Often called a "heller in skirts," she fascinated the public with her bronc-riding stunts. In a display of independence, Griffith boldly rode her favorite pony up the steps of Grant's Tomb during a Wild West show parade in New York. A delighted crowd wildly applauded her audacious act.

Lillian Ward was another daring bronco rider with the Amazons. Born in Brooklyn, New York, Lillian learned to ride after relocating to Texas while she was in her twenties. Her equestrian skills were discovered by Cody himself. After watching her ride a particularly disagreeable horse that most men refused to sit, Cody recruited her for his show.[304]

The most famous of the Amazons was a scrappy cowgirl from the East Coast named Adele Von Ohl Parker. In promotion material for his show, Cody noted that Adele was a "mixture of feminine delicacy and masculine will." Born on December 13, 1885, in Plainfield, New Jersey, she was determined to entertain audiences with her exceptional equestrienne talents. Her father was a rider with the New York Dragoons, a cavalry regiment with the Union army. Her mother and grandmother operated a riding school and trained horses. Adele, her sister, and brother were among the pupils who attended the respected academy.[305]

One of the first occasions Adele was written about in newspapers involved an encounter with a horse. She was attempting to ride a small bay bronco belonging to her brother down Park Avenue in New Jersey on Saturday evening July 18, 1903, when the animal became agitated and attempted to run away. The horse stumbled and fell and then became entangled in the harness. Passersby helped Adele free the animal from the knotted harness. The horse bucked and plunged a bit, but in the end, Adele got control, and the rider and bronco headed home.[306]

Simply saddling and riding her prized horse, Delmar, from one point to another would never do for Adele. She enjoyed riding fast and performing tricks on the back of her horse in the process. Adele would jump out of the saddle and back in again while riding at high speeds. She could even

Adele Von Ohl Parker at the conclusion of one of her performaces. BUFFALO BILL CENTER OF THE WEST, CODY, WYOMING; BUFFALO BILL MUSEUM; MS006-WILLIAM F. CODY COLLECTION; P.6.0398.

stand in the saddle and hold the position when the animal was cantering. She demonstrated her trick riding skills at several horse shows at Madison Square Garden.[307]

Adele was a favorite of horse show fans, both as an exhibitor and as a rider. Reporters referred to her as "a most charming example of the athletic girl" and followed her career religiously. "Her recent entry [in the Madison

Square Garden show] is Daisy, a white pony," the November 15, 1904, edition of the *Courier News* noted. "It is a handsome little equine, raised on the Von Ohl place. Its gifted and lovely owner is Miss Von Ohl Parker. It stands every chance of winning a blue ribbon.[308]

"Tomorrow Miss Von Ohl will ride a prize-winner in the combination class, for another exhibitor. She is a perfect horsewoman, and none of the horse's good points will suffer by reason of her riding.[309]

"While an enthusiastic believer in the doctrine of outdoors, and a steady follower of her belief, she is exceedingly prepossessing and graceful and as engaging in manner, as the most babyish of the old fashion 'clinging' type of girl.

"Not only does she excel as an equestrian, but she is an expert shot with the rifle, shotgun, and revolver and during the hunting season spends much of her time booted and short-skirted out after game. While she has not done much trapshooting, she is interested in the sport and may take part in the tournament of the Gun Club Saturday afternoon. The committee in charge of the shoot are exceedingly anxious to have Miss Von Ohl add to the general interest in the shoot by an appearance at the traps and have offered to put a special exhibition event on the program for a display of her skill. Miss Von Ohl, however, is not seeking notoriety and for that reason she hesitates to promise the gun club that she will

Adele Von Ohl Parker was an equestrienne, daredevil rider, vaudeville performer, and from 1929 to 1966 the owner and operator of Parker's Ranch in North Olmsted, Ohio. X-21929, THE DENVER PUBLIC LIBRARY, SPECIAL COLLECTIONS.

appear in a shoot where all the other participants are men. Should she take part, there is no doubt that she will make some of the crack shots in trousers work hard to equal her scores."[310]

In a short time, Adele's talent grew beyond what could be included in horse shows, and the trick rider and bronc buster was hired to perform at the Hippodrome in New York. Adele was billed as the "fair maid from Texas" because producers for the Western show Adele was to star in believed patrons would prefer seeing a girl from Texas rather than New Jersey. The April 25, 1905, edition of the *Buffalo Courier* described the girl equestrienne in glowing terms. "She is a cowgirl with a complexion of peaches and cream, pretty as you like, with dancing black eyes…. Adele's long suit is doing things with horses - the meaner the better. She did things in yesterday's show that made people sit up and wonder what sort of girl this young person could be. She lariated a kicking stallion from her little pony, clapped a saddle on him before he knew what happened, and was riding him around the ring, clinging like glue, while he raved and racked and tied himself up into knots. Then she shied her sombrero into the ring, hung from the saddle with one foot in the stirrup, and caught up with the hat as easy as a cowboy."[311]

The riding and roping demonstration Adele offered at the Hippodrome was incorporated into the part the entertainer was playing at the theater. She took on a comedic role in the show about an unsophisticated country girl who stays with her rich, proper relatives in the city. Laughter ensued when Adele's character tried to teach one of her cultured cousins how to ride a horse. Adele had to pretend the horse was spooked at some point during the performance and had to ride the animal until she brought it under control. In late October 1905, that scene was to be filmed in a park near the Hippodrome. The finished product was to be shown at Nickelodeon theaters from coast to coast.[312]

The production did not go as planned, however, and Adele nearly lost her life. The make-believe rescue of the horse became an episode fraught with danger when Adele's skirt got caught on the pommel of the saddle and she fell sideways, her foot still in the harness. She was unable to lift herself out of the saddle and stop the horse from running. The animal was truly frightened by what was happening and had gone wild. A mounted police officer managed to overtake the horse and, leaning down, grabbed Adele and swung her up in front of him on his own horse.[313]

The camera captured the harrowing incident from start to finish, and it was featured at Nickelodeon theaters everywhere. Patrons had no idea the drama was real. As a result, Adele was a horseback riding sensation long before screen stars Tom Mix or William S. Hart made their first film.

In addition to the tricks she performed in the saddle in various comedies, Adele appeared with her horse in a handful of tragedies as well. At the conclusion of a Civil War drama, she and her ride would dive off a high platform into a pool below. Audiences erupted in applause at the daring feat. The perfect execution of the death-defying stunt earned Adele the title of "America's Most Daring Woman Rider."[314]

Adele aspired to be an accomplished actress. At seventeen, she was performing dramatic sketches at posh venues like the Hotel Netherwood in Plainfield. She wanted to excel on stage acting as much as she did in the saddle riding. Toward that end, she attended acting classes and received voice training from reputable New York voice coaches. Just where her career would take her she didn't know, but she wanted to be prepared.[315]

When Buffalo Bill Cody, arguably the most famous Wild West show producer in the history of such programs, heard about Adele, he hurried to hire her to work for him. Adele officially joined Buffalo Bill's cast in the spring of 1907. The show was touring the East Coast, and those in the region familiar with the daring rider's routine flocked to see her. Cody's cast of thrill-seeking women captivated audiences. Young girls admired cowgirls like Adele—women who broke away from society's traditional roles, jumped aboard a horse, and held their own in a predominantly male profession. Adele was aware of the impact she had on those young female fans and took every opportunity to prove to them there was nothing a woman couldn't do.[316]

On April 13, 1908, she took to the streets of Broadway on her horse to promote the ladies in the Wild West show who had saddled up and followed their dreams. Adele rode her horse down the busiest thoroughfare in New York City on her way to join her fellow female cast members waiting to perform in Bridgeport, Connecticut.[317]

When Adele wasn't on the road with Cody's show, she was home performing on stage in various plays. In late spring 1908, she starred in a farce comedy titled *A Box of Monkeys*, in which she offered a humorous monologue and entertained the audience by singing a couple of popular songs.[318]

New Jersey residents anxious for their star to return to Plainfield to stay for a while were thrilled to learn Adele would be heading East from Memphis at the close of her engagement with Cody's program. Members of the press were waiting to interview her when she stepped off the Atlantic Coast Line steamer in New York on December 3, 1908.[319]

"Traveling over 22,000 miles in thirty weeks, Miss Adele Von Ohl, returned home yesterday, enthusiastic about her wonderful experience as a member of Buffalo Bill's Wild West show," the December 4, 1908, edition of the *Central New Jersey Home News* reported. "After exhibiting for three weeks last May at Madison Square Garden, the show traveled through Pennsylvania, and then jumped to the Eastern states going as far north as Maine, then on to the middle states as far as St. Louis…."[320]

"Miss Von Ohl appeared at every performance on her celebrated pony Aristocrat, who executes many wonderful stunts, including the cake walk, that of jumping three feet into the air from a standing position and many other tricks which the owner describes as of the high school variety. Everywhere both rider and animal received a great ovation."[321]

Among the cast members Adele met touring with Buffalo Bill Cody's Wild West show was a bronc riding performer named James Letcher Parker. Born in Cheyenne, Wyoming, on October 26, 1886, Parker was a lawyer prior to working in rodeos. The pair bonded over their mutual love of horses and travel. They married on July 29, 1909, in Kankakee County, Illinois. The Parkers remained with Cody's show through the first year of their marriage.[322]

In early 1911, the couple decided to join the vaudeville circuit and performed with Arizona Joe and Company in a series of Wild West shows titled *A Glimpse of Prairie Life and Cheyenne Days*. Replete with thrilling acts that illustrated life on the plains, Adele was billed as the "Noted Wyoming Horse Woman" and performed with her high school broncos Ditmar and Diablo. The show and the star riders were well received and critically praised from Tacoma, Washington, to Tulsa, Oklahoma.[323]

"All the audience needs to do to imagine themselves looking out of the ranch window and watching the cowboys and cowgirls in the evening frolicking with their horses, is to pay no attention to the walls and the lights, etc. of the theater," the April 29, 1912, edition of the *New York Times* boasted about the Wild West show.[324]

"Those who haven't seen the great act by Adele Von Ohl should make every effort to do so," an article in the January 8, 1912, edition of the *Press Sun Bulletin* announced.[325]

In the summer of 1913, Adele, her husband, and the rest of the cast of Arizona Joe and Company traveled overseas to perform for audiences in some of the most notable theaters in Europe. Not all of Adele's time would be spent working on stage. She had a legal matter to attend to in England and, if all went as planned, the Parkers expected to return to America as millionaires.[326]

Sir Benjamin Laing Stites of Dundee, a distant relative of the Von Ohls, left an $8 million estate to be divided among his relatives. Adele made arrangements to meet with Sir Stites' solicitors and lay claim to her portion of the fortune. The cowgirl actress hoped to use some of the money to produce her own Wild West show.[327]

Adele and her husband returned to New Jersey on December 27, 1913. The Wild West programs had been successful and well attended. Adele celebrated both the positive response she received from European audiences and the small fortune she inherited.

Between 1914 and 1916, Adele lent her talent to several shows. Now billed as the "Champion Lady Bronco Buster of the World," she appeared at the Strand Theatre on Broadway, the Bowdoin Square Theatre in Boston, and the Pantages Theatres in San Francisco and Los Angeles. Theatregoers marveled at the way she handled a horse. She credited her parents for her ability to break wild horses. They had taught her how to train horses, and the prowess had become a passion.[328]

When the United States was contemplating entering World War I in 1916, Adele made a suggestion to government officials to put Red Cross nurses working in the field on horseback. She offered to do the training for the mission. The radical idea made the front page of newspapers across the country.[329]

"Here is the latest new project under the sun which is being wished upon Los Angeles by a woman who has been nurse, equestrienne, and society woman, by turn," an article in the July 13, 1916, edition of the *Los Angeles Record* read. "And why haven't we thought of the plan before, you'll all say when you know the details. The idea originated in the clever brain of Adele Von Ohl who appears in a riding act at the Pantages this week.[330]

"'I think there are always many women who are living a social butterfly existence,' said Miss Von Ohl today, 'who would dearly love to go in for something worthwhile. The present war has awakened the spirit of doing among a number of rich women who have gone to the front in the service of the Red Cross. I think a great many more could be interested in this wonderfully human peculiarly woman's work, if it were promoted in times of peace and in countries at peace as well as at war.[331]

"'…I am in favor of the Red Cross mounted brigade being organized in every city in the country. I think the women who enter it might very well be women who are interested in doing something for others.

"'They might not only become proficient as horsewomen, but they might be equally capable of handling a machine or driving a team…. I should like to see this organization of women make itself a first aid, not only in time of war to the soldier but in time of peace to the civilian, and it could answer emergency calls, such as in accidents, fires, or riots. Often on such occasions there is grave need of a woman's hand and a woman's care.'[332]

"Miss Von Ohl so firmly believes in her plan that she took the matter up with the Out West Riding Club in Los Angeles and continues her propaganda everywhere she goes."[333]

The years between 1917 and 1928 were filled with stage performances, dazzling crowds with fancy and trick riding exhibitions and bronc busting demonstrations. The expert horsewoman was renowned from the Atlantic to the Pacific. When motion pictures became the rage, she was sought after by film producers wanting her to be a stuntwoman in a series of Western films. She worked alongside some of the most popular film stars of the day, including Hoot Gibson and Buck Jones.[334]

By this time in her life she had two daughters. No matter how busy Adele was with work and her family, she always found time to participate in horse shows. At the California Stock Horse Classic in April 1923, she rode a buckskin gelding to victory on three consecutive nights. She won first place trophies and one second place award.[335]

Adele joined the cast of Wild West entertainers with Ringling Bros. and Barnum & Bailey in the spring of 1928. At the age of forty-three she was still performing bold stunts on the back of a horse. She brought audiences to their feet at Madison Square Garden with tricks known as the pickup and the death drag. The pickup involved leaning low, almost sideways in the saddle, to retrieve a kerchief on the floor of the arena. The death drag was a stunt where the rider hung upside down on the side of the horse as it galloped at full speed. Adele was among the first women to perform either stunt in a show.[336]

Shortly after Adele's mother died in May 1928, she decided to retire from working in vaudeville, circuses, and Wild West shows and turned her attention to establishing a riding school in Cleveland, Ohio. The Von Ohl Equestrian School opened for business in the fall of 1928. Adele believed northeast Ohio was the perfect location for her school of horsemanship because, according to her, the Rocky River Valley "provided the grandest riding range in the United States." She eventually moved the school to North Olmsted, Ohio, on a six-acre parcel of land and changed the name of the learning institution to Parker's Ranch. In addition to teaching students how to ride and sit properly in a saddle, she also taught them how to swim horses. Adele's pupils were given a chance to demonstrate what they'd learned at the school by participating in the horse shows she produced at the ranch in which the public was invited to attend.[337]

In an interview Adele did with the Great Falls, Montana newspaper, the *Great Falls Tribune*, in April 1965, she admitted that if she could live anywhere other than Ohio it would be in Montana. At one time she and her husband had had a ranch in Sheridan, Montana, and she had fallen in love with the state. She told the *Great Falls Tribune* reporter that Cleveland was home because "the services of a horsewoman are more in demand in a heavily populated part of the country."[338]

For more than thirty years, Adele contented herself with running the equestrian school and reliving her days touring the United States and Europe by performing with her many students.[339]

The avid horsewoman and equestrian instructor passed away on January 21, 1966, at the age of eighty. More than three hundred of her pupils attended the funeral. She was laid to rest at the Brook Avenue Presbyterian Cemetery in North Plainfield, New Jersey.[340] ✎

PART 11

TRICK ROPING

LIBRARY OF CONGRESS

Alice Sisty

A hush fell over the large crowd at the rodeo arena in Salt Lake City, Utah, in July 1938 as daredevil rider Alice Sisty raced into the arena atop two English jumpers. She was standing on the backs of the animals with one foot on one horse and the other foot on the second mount, known as Roman riding. Alice led the horses into a gallop around the arena as the audience cheered and applauded. She expertly handled the jumpers named Whale and Brownstone. Alice had performed the Roman standard jump a number of times and was confident the trick would come off perfectly.

The trick involved the excited horses leaping over a parked automobile. It was an outstanding feat that, when executed well, brought rodeo fans out of their seats shouting for joy. Alice did not disappoint. Her signature jump was flawlessly carried out. She waved to the wildly cheering audience as she urged her horses into another pass at the stunt.

Born in Netcong, New Jersey, in January 1913, Alice first broke into national headlines when, at twenty years of age, she rode an Indian pony from

Alice Sisty was a trick roper and trick rider who stunned crowds across the nation. COURTESY OF COWGIRL MAGAZINE.

Reno, Nevada, to the steps of New York City Hall. It was a three-thousand mile journey, and, when she arrived in New York, mayors from coast to coast celebrated Alice's accomplishment with letters of congratulations. The Cheyenne, Wyoming, Chamber of Commerce helped defray Alice's expenses on the journey, and she helped advertise the Cheyenne Frontier Days by wearing a cowboy suit with the Cheyenne inscription on its back.

Alice had been riding horses since the age of six. Her grandfather owned a racetrack, and the love of horses was undoubtedly born in her. One of Alice's first rodeo appearances was in Asbury Park. It was followed by well-received appearances in such places as Des Moines, Iowa; Cheyenne, Wyoming; Omaha, Nebraska; and Billings, Montana. She performed at the Chicago World's Fair and at Madison Square Garden.

Billed as a trick and fancy rider, Alice won numerous cowgirl championships. She was one of the highest-paid female rodeo performers in the 1930s. Friends and fans seldom, if ever, saw her without her makeup and hair done to perfection and adorned in beautiful cowgirl clothing. The dark-haired, blue-eyed Alice had decided to become a cowgirl when she was nineteen and signed to ride in Colonel Zack Millers' 101 Ranch Wild West Show.

In addition to the prized English jumpers with which she used to perform the Roman standard jump trick, she owned a white Arabian horse named Chopa. Chopa was a highly intelligent animal that responded to every command of Alice's voice. The pair were seen together in rodeo shows from coast to coast.

Alice passed away from an unnamed illness on September 11, 1953, in Crescent City, California, where she lived with her second husband, Hennie Sommer. Alice was forty years old when she died. ❖

The Parry Sisters

A strong gust of wind blew a pair of tumbleweeds into the path of a team of horses hitched to a wagon. It spooked the animals, and they reared and bucked and then bolted. The gray-haired woman holding the reins of the team screamed. The wagon pitched and swayed as the horses jerked it around. The woman cried out for help.

Suddenly, a magnificent stallion raced toward the out of control wagon. The confident rider, adorned in buckskin britches and a jacket, spurred the stallion along until it caught up to the team. Springing forward, the rider leapt out of the saddle and landed on the back of one of the horses.

The brave rider swerved the team out of the path of a group of townspeople just as they were leaving church. A shout went up from the onlookers. The lady driving the wagon regained her composure and pulled back on the reins. The daring horseback rider helped quiet the team to a stop.

A thunderous round of applause echoed around them. The lady in the wagon stood up, removed the gray wig on her head, and took a bow. The rider dismounted, removed her cowboy hat, and waved to the crowd of spectators. The audience that had assembled to witness the performance in Buffalo Bill Cody's Wild West show was not disappointed by the expert display of horsemanship exhibited by the high riding Parry sisters.[341]

Etheyle and Juanita Parry were often billed as the Parry Twins during their short, but illustrious, careers as Wild West performers and rodeo riders. The pair was, however, born a year apart. Their father, veterinarian Archer E. Parry, and the sisters' mother, Amy Rothermel Parry, were residents of Riverside, New York. Their first daughter, Etheyle, was born on April 18, 1889, and she was named after the chemical compound ethyl-chloride. Dr. Parry had been experimenting with the substance, which was similar to Novocain, for use on horses. He thought the word ethyl would make a good name. Juanita was born on September 20, 1890.[342]

The Parry Sisters were two of the most daring riders to perform in Buffalo Bill Cody's Wild West show. BUFFALO BILL CENTER OF THE WEST, CODY, WYOMING; BUFFALO BILL MUSEUM; MS006-WILLIAM F. CODY COLLECTION; P.69.1285.2

Dr. Parry's love for animals, particularly horses, was inherited by his daughters. Born in Denver, Dr. Parry, in his younger life, had been a cowboy, working on a ranch roping cattle and doing all the other jobs known to cowhands. During his employment at the ranch, he became friends with two other men working at the same location, Theodore Roosevelt and William F. Cody. Dr. Parry taught Etheyle and Juanita all he knew about horses, including how best to care for them. Both young women were exceptional horseback riders. Their talent in the saddle was recognized by Bill Cody, who visited the Parrys regularly. In 1907, when the Parry sisters were seventeen and sixteen years old, Cody invited them to join his Wild West show.[343]

Buffalo Bill's Wild West show was a leading source of entertainment in the early 1900s. During that time of worldwide travel and countless presentations, a myriad of performers captured the hearts and imaginations of fans everywhere. The Parry sisters were part of a sizable cast of thrill-seeking women who captivated audiences in the United States and abroad. For more than four years, Etheyle and Juanita honed their riding skills and became one of the top acts for Cody's program. Some of the trick riding routines they presented involved the pair riding side by side into an arena and leaping from one horse to the other at full gallop. Among the cast and crew, the sisters were called the Cossack Girls because they performed all the reckless and daring feats of horsemanship attributed to the Russian Cossack cavalrymen.[344]

In December 1910, the sisters returned to New York to attend their father's funeral. Dr. Parry had suffered a stroke earlier in the year and died of complications as a result. In addition to losing their father, Etheyle and Juanita had to say goodbye to the men and women they'd come to know while working for Cody's Wild West show. Cody had announced he would be retiring, and the Parrys needed to find another show to join. By February 1911, the women had signed a contract with the Miller Brothers 101 Ranch Wild West show.[345]

Cowgirls were an important part of the popular Wild West show out of Oklahoma. The cast included many well-known riders, ropers, and crack rifle shots. The May 10, 1912, edition of the *Butte Miner* noted the many talented female acts involved with the show. "There is, for instance, Lulu B. Parr, who last season accepted a dare to ride a wild horse in Philadelphia, and despite the fact that she was nearly killed, owing to the breaking of her saddle girth, pluckily attempted the feat again the next day and succeeded in thoroughly taming the vicious animal," the newspaper article read. "There is Tillie Baldwin, a real ranch girl, who was entered at the recent rodeo in Los Angeles as an 'unknown,' and carried off all the prizes for lady riders of unbroken broncos. There is Etheyle Parry, whose name suggests the footlights and Broadway, but who is nevertheless a real cowgirl and has won several prizes for her cleverness as a rough rider at the annual roundups at Bliss, Oklahoma, Cheyenne, and Pendleton."[346]

When they weren't performing, both Etheyle and Juanita competed in rodeos. They participated in roping and bronc riding events, adding various trophies to their long list of accolades. The Parry women looked enough alike to be called twins, and stories about the two carried in newspapers across the country often remarked how unusual it was for the two to be so similar and not be twins. In an interview with the *Seattle Star* on May 21, 1912, the sisters were quoted as saying, "We have a great deal in common, but are very different people." Among the things the pair had in common, the article explained, "is the fact that they have always lived on ranches and would rather ride horseback than in the finest and swiftest auto in the world."[347]

Various newspaper articles about the 101 Ranch Wild West show often included stories about the women within the cast competing for best lady rider of bucking horses. Etheyle was often listed in a contest for the title with accomplished cowgirls Tillie Baldwin and Lulu Parr. "These girls are all clever and daring riders," the July 27, 1912, edition of the *Des Moines Tribune* reported. "They do stunts in the big show that make the ordinary cowboy hesitate. They ride 'outlaw' horses, they lasso wild ponies, they dash around the arena on long horned steers, and they perform other feats that make the eyes of the spectators open wide and sends the blood circulating through the veins with a mixture of fear and admiration."[348]

Juanita and Etheyle kept the routine they used in the Wild West show fresh with new tricks. Not only did they not want the audience to become bored with their act, but they also didn't want to become bored either. In the summer of 1913, they perfected a trick that involved picking up items scattered across a performance arena. After a variety of objects (ranging from a

Juanita Parry riding her paint horse into the rodeo arena. BUFFALO BILL CENTER OF THE WEST, CODY, WYOMING; BUFFALO BILL MUSEUM; MS006-WILLIAM F. CODY COLLECTION; P.69.2080

Etheyle Parry mounted on one of her favorite horses. BUFFALO BILL CENTER OF THE WEST, CODY, WYOMING; BUFFALO BILL MUSEUM; MS006-WILLIAM F. CODY COLLECTION; P.69.1905

handkerchief to a lasso) were placed on the ground, the women would race their horses toward those items. When they got close enough to the objects, the sisters would lean over in their saddles and scoop them up. The trick ended with Juanita sitting on the ground in the arena and Etheyle spurring her horse toward her. Just when it looked like Juanita would be trampled, she would raise her arms high, and Etheyle would grab her sister up and toss her on the back of her saddle.[349]

The Parry sisters received top billing at the 101 Ranch Wild West show exhibition in Ottumwa, Iowa, in late summer 1913. One of the highlights of the show was an illustration of an attack on a train of prairie schooners by hostile Indians. Etheyle and Juanita played the part of settlers trying to gain control of frightened teams of horses pulling a pair of schooners. "These Oklahoma girls have been expert riders since they were children," a Decatur, Illinois, newspaper noted about the Parry sisters. (Because the 101 Ranch was located in Oklahoma, reporters often wrote that the various acts were from that area.) "[The Parry sisters] are equally at home on high school horses or on outlaw broncos, and they excel in roping, picking up articles from the ground while riding at breakneck speed and in all other sports of the range and prairie. Withal, the twins are pretty and attractive, and are good to look at, on or off a horse."[350]

Both Etheyle and Juanita were experts with the lariat. The Parrys, in addition to five other women with the 101 Ranch Wild West show, were seven of the best female lariat throwers in the world. The Parry sisters were top among the seven, with Etheyle being the better of the two. She had the distinction of being the only woman who could swing a lariat 110 feet in length.[351]

Etheyle and Juanita's careers with the 101 Ranch Wild West show spanned more than four years. When they weren't traveling with the show, they spent time at the Miller Brothers' ranch in Bliss, Oklahoma. While there, they practiced their act and performed in several silent Western pictures starring Broncho Billy Anderson and Tom Mix.[352]

In the fall of 1916, the Parrys signed a contract with the Barnum & Bailey Circus. The circus produced its own Wild West show, and Etheyle and Juanita were part of that cast. The pair performed in every major city across the country. Not only were they celebrated for their daring feats of horse-manship, but also for the elaborate velvet costumes they wore in their act. Their hats, neckerchiefs, gauntlet gloves, and beaded armbands were equally impressive and admired.[353]

On September 7, 1917, the Parry sisters were center stage performing before a sold-out crowd in Chicago. Riding bareback, Juanita was executing one of the duo's most difficult tricks, a double somersault on the back of the horse, when her mount stumbled and fell. Juanita was pinned under the animal. Her neck was broken, and her skull was crushed. She died two days later.[354]

Etheyle Parry escorted her sister's body back to New York, and Juanita was buried beside her father at the Kenesco Cemetery in Westchester County. Heartbroken by the experience, Etheyle retired from the Wild West show profession. More than three years after the passing of her sister, Etheyle married Buffalo Bill Cody's nephew, William Cody Bradford. William had been born in 1872, and he and Etheyle had met when they were younger. The couple was wed on February 28, 1921, in Casper, Wyoming. The March 1, 1921, edition of the *Casper Daily Tribune* carried a story about the nuptials. The ceremony was performed by Reverend Charles A. Wilson at the groom's house in Casper where he was employed with the Northwestern Railroad. Their friends, Mr. and Mrs. Earl Rager, were the only guests and served as best man and matron of honor.[355]

The Bradfords were happily married for more than twelve years. William was a well-respected executive and Etheyle an artist whose paintings had been featured in exhibits throughout the state of Wyoming. In late 1932, William began struggling with his health, and a negative diagnosis brought about serious depression. On September 4, 1933, he shot himself to death. William was sixty years old.[356]

Etheyle Parry Bradford passed away on May 14, 1962, at the age of seventy-three. She was laid to rest beside her sister Juanita.[357]

ENDNOTES

Steer Roping

[1] *The Livestock Inspector*, October 15, 1899
[2] *America's First Cowgirl*, pg. 66-67
[3] The *El Paso Herald*, July 21, 1900
[4] *Mountain Gazette*, December 10, 1960
[5] The *St. Louis Republic*, May 17, 1901
[6] *Lucille Mulhall: Wild West Cowgirl*, pg. 125-126, *America's First Cowgirl*, pg. 66-67
[7] *America's First Cowgirl*, pg. 83-86
[8] Ibid.
[9] The *Pryor Creek Clipper*, May 17, 1901
[10] The *El Paso Herald*, December 20, 1902
[11] *America's First Cowgirl*, pg. 108-109
[13] Ibid., The *El Paso Herald*, December 20, 1902
[14] *Claflin Clarion*, January 29, 1903, The *Neihart Herald*, February 12, 1903, Oklahoma Rodeo Women, pg. 33-34
[15] The *Butte Miner*, April 19, 1903
[16] Ibid.
[17] Ibid.
[18] Ibid.
[19] The *St. Louis Dispatch*, January 18, 1907
[20] The *Kansas City Star*, January 21, 1907
[21] *America's First Cowgirl*, pg. 160-162
[22] *America's First Cowgirl*, pg. 163-165
[23] Ibid.
[24] The *Chicago Livestock World*, May 19, 1910
[25] Ibid.
[26] Ibid.
[27] *Manitoba Free Press*, March 31, 1914
[28] Ibid.
[29] *America's First Cowgirl*, pg. 132-133
[30] The *Haworth Herald*, May 9, 1919, *Star Tribune*, May 29, 1922
[31] *America's First Cowgirl*, pg. 156-157
[32] *Lubbock Morning Avalanche*, December 24, 1940, The *Daily Oklahoman*, December 27, 1940
[33] The *Livestock Inspector*, October 15, 1899
[34] The *Daily Oklahoman*, December 27, 1940

Bulldogging

[35] *Fort Worth Star-Telegram*, November 2, 1924
[36] The *Sacramento Bee*, September 12, 1912, The *Sacramento Bee*, September 20, 1912
[37] https://sites.rootsweb.com/~ksbarber/hastings_fox.html
[38] The *Standard Union*, August 1, 1916
[39] The *Standard Union*, August 8, 1916

[40] *Calgary Herald*, July 13, 1917

[41] The *Standard Union*, August 1, 1916

[42] Ibid.

[43] *Calgary Herald*, July 13, 1917

[44] *Barber County Index*, August 30, 1923,
   http://sites.rootsweb.com/ksbarber/massey-joe-modainroundup.html

[45] *Joplin Globe*, September 27, 1923

[46] The *Galveston Daily News*, March 24, 1924

[47] Ibid.

[48] The *Daily Deadwood Pioneer Times*, June 7, 1924, *Fort Worth Star-Telegram*,
   April 16, 1924, *Bristow Daily Record*, May 8, 1924

[49] The *Daily Deadwood Pioneer Times*, June 7, 1924

[50] The *Daily Deadwood Pioneer Times*, July 2, 1924, The *News Review*, September 19, 1924

[51] *North Adams Transit*, October 30, 1924, The *Kansas City Times*, December 12, 1924,
   Arizona Daily Star, February 21, 1925

[52] The *Vernon Record*, February 10, 1925, *Fort Worth Star-Telegram*, February 5, 1925

[53] *Fort Worth Star-Telegram*, March 11, 1925

[54] The *Gazette*, June 19, 1925

[55] The *Ardmore Daily Press*, July 26, 1925

[56] Ibid.

[57] Ibid.

[58] The *Burwell Tribune*, August 6, 1925

[59] *Los Angeles Times*, October 23, 1925

[60] *Fort Worth Record-Telegram*, March 10, 1926

[61] *Coweta Times Star*, June 30, 1926

[62] The *Philadelphia Inquirer*, July 4, 1926

[63] Ibid.

[64] Ibid.

[65] *Daily News*, November 4, 1927

[66] The *Waco News Tribune*, October 15, 1929, *El Paso Evening News*, September 23, 1929

[67] *El Paso Evening News*, September 27, 1929

[68] The *Tucson Citizen*, January 29, 1936

[69] *Napa Journal*, April 19, 1936

[70] Ibid.

[71] The *Arizona Republic*, August 1, 1948, The *Arizona Republic*, August 15, 1948

[72] The *Arizona Republic*, August 15, 1948, www.ancestry.com Charlie C. Wilson

Bronc Riding

[73] *Casper Star Tribune*, March 1, 1933, *Casper Star Tribune*, February 10, 1933

[74] *Casper Star Tribune*, March 1, 1933

[75] *Jackson Hole Courier*, March 2, 1933

[76] *Jackson Hole Courier*, April 6, 1933

[77] The *Pinedale Roundup*, June 8, 1933

[78] www.ancestry.com Rosa Belle "Prairie Rose Henderson" Gale

[79] The *Custer County Chief*, October 6, 1893

80 *Natrona County Tribune*, October 14, 1897, *Crook County Monitor*, September 1, 1899
81 www.ancestry.com Rosa Belle "Prairie Rose Henderson" Gale
82 The *Hutchinson Gazette*, August 5, 1919
83 *El Paso Times*, March 6, 1912
84 The *Arizona Republic*, February 17, 1912, *Lead Daily Call*, August 9, 1912,
    Tribune Stockman Farmer, August 20, 1912
85 The *Topeka Daily Capital*, September 12, 1912
86 *Los Angeles Evening Express*, February 18, 1913, *Sioux City Journal*, June 22, 1913
87 *Sioux City Journal*, July 3, 1913
88 *Frank Leslie's Illustrated Newspaper*, July 21, 1913, *Vern County News*, July 23, 1913
89 The *Winnipeg Tribune*, August 14, 1913, *East Oregonian*, September 12, 1914,
    The *Spokesman Review*, September 18, 1914, The *Spokesman Review*, September 20, 1914
90 www.abioh.byui.edu/specialcollections/westernstates/westernstatesrecorddetails.cfm
91 The *Skiatook News*, April 28, 1915, The *Evening Sun*, May 12, 1915
92 The *Salt Lake Tribune*, October 6, 1915
93 *Douglass Tribune*, January 28, 1916, *Boston Post*, August 20, 1916,
    Encampment Record, August 9, 1917, *Albany Daily Democrat*, August 29, 1917
94 *Cheyenne State Leader*, March 5, 1919
95 *Palladium Item*, May 30, 1919, The *Indianapolis Star*, May 22, 1919,
    The *Garden City Telegram*, August 7, 1919
96 The *Tiller and Toiler*, September 30, 1920
97 The *Hutchinson Gazette*, May 31, 1920
98 Ibid.
99 *Casper Star Tribune*, March 3, 1933, *Casper Star Tribune*, August 25, 1929
100 *Casper Star Tribune*, March 9, 1933
101 *Casper Star Tribune*, July 26, 1939
102 *Casper Star Tribune*, October 22, 1939

Trick Shooting

103 *The Times*, June 10, 1885
104 *Pawnee Bill: A Biography of Major Gordon Lillie*, pg. 100-101
105 *Pawnee Bill: A Biography of Major Gordon Lillie*, pg. 73, 100-101
106 Ibid.
107 The *Evening Telegram*, September 1, 1886
108 *Pawnee Bill: A Biography of Major Gordon Lillie*, pg. 116-117
109 Ibid.
110 Ibid.
111 Ibid.
112 Ibid.
113 The *Peabody Weekly Republican*, September 16, 1887
114 The *Boston Journal*, December 10, 1887
115 *Pawnee Bill: A Biography of Major Gordon Lillie*, pg. 117-118
116 *Ashland Weekly News*, August 7, 1889
117 *Oakland Tribune*, January 15, 1928
118 *Pawnee Bill: A Biography of Major Gordon Lillie*, pg. 199-200, 174-175, 180-181

[119] The *Joliet News*, June 6, 1907
[120] Ibid.
[121] Ibid.
[122] Ibid.
[123] The *Weekly Kansas City Star*, September 23, 1936
[124] *Pawnee Bill: A Biography of Major Gordon Lillie*, pg. 122-124
[125] The *El Reno Daily Tribune*, August 31, 1936
[126] Ibid.
[127] The *Weekly Kansas City Star*, September 23, 1936
[128] The *Rock Island Argus*, September 22, 1936

Hobbled Stirrup Riding

[129] *Elmore County Republican*, September 7, 1912, *Los Angeles Express*, March 25, 1912
[130] *Hartford Courant*, August 23, 1925
[131] *Hartford Courant*, October 19, 1930
[132] Ibid.
[133] Ibid.
[134] Ibid.
[135] Ibid.
[136] *Monterey Daily Cypress*, January 11, 1913
[137] The *Tacoma Times*, July 3, 1913, The *Winnipeg Tribune*, August 15, 1913,
The *Spokesman Review*, August 2, 1913
[138] The *Times*, September 10, 1916
[139] Ibid.
[140] *Fitchburg Sentinel*, September 28, 1917, The *Manchester Journal*, September 2, 1920,
Norwich Bulletin, May 26, 1917
[141] *Calgary Herald*, August 28, 1919
[142] *Bennington Banner*, September 10, 1920, The *Boston Globe*, September 28, 1921,
Independent Observer, June 21, 1923
[143] *Independent Observer*, June 21, 1923
[144] *Hartford Courant*, August 23, 1925
[145] Ibid.
[146] Ibid.
[147] Ibid.
[148] *Hartford Courant*, August 18, 1957
[149] *Hartford Courant*, February 4, 1935
[150] The *Oklahoma News*, August 18, 1935
[151] *Daily News*, August 23, 1936
[152] *Scranton Tribune*, September 29. 1946
[153] *Hartford Courant*, August 18, 1957

Trick Riding

[154] The *Caney Daily Chronicle*, October 22, 1920, The *Ottawa Herald*, August 4, 1920
[155] The *Ottawa Herald*, August 4, 1920, The *Caney Daily Chronicle*, October 22, 1920
[156] www.ancestry.com Hazel Hickey, Moore Family Records

157 Moore Family Records
158 Ibid.
159 Ibid.
160 Ibid.
161 Ibid.
162 The *Beemer Times*, June 14, 1923
163 The *News Herald*, May 24, 1924
164 The *Evening Times*, August 23, 1924, The *Davidsonian*, October 9, 1924, The *Evening Times*, August 16, 1924
165 *Dubuque Telegraph Herald*, May 13, 1926
166 *Bangor Daily News*, July 6, 1926
167 The *Evening Standard*, April 28, 1927
168 Ibid.
169 The *Dayton Herald*, April 30, 1928
170 The *Tampa Times*, December 2, 1927
171 Moore Family Records, *Times Union*, May 14, 1932, *Des Moines Tribune*, July 25, 1935, The *Boscobel Dial*, March 9, 2000
172 *Democrat and Chronicle*, June 28, 1937
173 Ibid.
174 *Big Country Journal*, September 8, 2019
175 *Clarion Ledger*, October 7, 1939
176 Ibid.
177 Moore Family Records
178 Ibid.
179 Ibid.
180 Ibid.
181 Ibid.
182 Ibid.

Rough Riding

183 *Harrisburg Telegram*, July 23, 1917
184 www.ancestry.com Lulu Bell Parr
185 *Elwood Daily Press*, September 23, 1895, *Delphos Daily Herald*, September 25, 1895
186 www.ancestry.com Lulu Bell Parr
187 Ibid.
188 The *Pittsburgh Press*, May 3, 1903
189 *Pittston Gazette*, July 24, 1906
190 The *Standard Union*, June 24, 1906
191 Ibid.
192 Ibid.
193 Ibid.
194 The *Philadelphia Inquirer*, June 7, 1908
195 The *Salt Lake Herald Republican*, November 30, 1908
196 The *Brooklyn Citizen*, May 21, 1910
197 Ibid.

[198] Ibid.

[199] *New Orleans Republican*, August 24, 1873

[200] *The Courier*, August 11, 1911

[201] Ibid.

[202] Ibid.

[203] Ibid.

[204] *Evening Times Republican*, July 27, 1912

[205] Ibid.

[206] Ibid.

[207] https://www.history.pcusa.org/services/records-management/records-congregations U.S. Presbyterian Church Records, 1896-1943, *Muskogee Daily Phoenix*, November 24, 1914, The *Times Democrat*, November 24, 1914

[208] *Billboard Magazine*, February 21, 1914

[209] Buffalo Bill Wild West Collection at the Center of the West MS 261 Lulu Bell

[210] Ibid.

[211] Ibid.

[212] *Weekly Journal Miner*, May 26, 1915

[213] *Pittsburgh Daily Post*, July 16, 1916

[214] *Weekly Journal Miner*, May 26, 1915

[215] Buffalo Bill Wild West Collection at the Center of the West MS 261 Lulu Bell

[216] Ibid.

[217] *Billboard Magazine*, April 4, 1921

[218] *Florence Morning News*, October 20, 1925

[219] *Billboard Magazine*, August 29, 1929

[220] The *La Crosse Tribune*, July 4, 1926

[221] Ibid.

[222] *Billboard Magazine*, June 4, 1927

[223] *Billboard Magazine*, March 23, 1929

[224] *Dodge City Journal*, September 19, 1929

[225] *Battle Creek Enquirer*, July 12, 1930

[226] The *Gazette and Daily*, May 17, 1938, *Dodge City Journal*, September 19, 1929

[227] *Dayton Daily News*, May 10, 2001

[228] *Argus Leader*, January 18, 1955, The *Spokesman Review*, January 19, 1955

[229] *Argus Leader*, January 18, 1955, The *Spokesman Review*, January 19, 1955

[230] *Argus Leader*, January 18, 1955, The *Spokesman Review*, January 19, 1955

Calf Roping

[231] *Fort Worth Star-Telegram*, March 12, 1922

[232] Ibid.

[233] Ibid.

[234] Ibid.

[235] *Fort Worth Record-Telegram*, March 27, 1922

[236] www.ancestry.com Ruth Roach Salmon

[237] The *Kansas City Times*, May 25, 1912

[238] *Billboard Magazine*, March 22, 1913

[239] The *Hugo Husonian*, June 5, 1913

[240] *El Dorado Republican*, November 13, 1916

[241] www.ancestry.com Ruth Roach Salmon, The *Democrat Opinion*, August 10, 1917

[242] *Fort Worth Star-Telegram*, March 13, 1917, *El Paso Times*, March 11, 1917, *Valley Morning Star*, October 24, 2010

[243] *Fort Worth Star-Telegram*, March 13, 1919

[244] Ibid.

[245] *Fort Worth Star-Telegram*, April 10, 1919

[246] Ibid.

[247] The *Chickasha Star*, February 13, 1920, *Fort Worth Star-Telegram*, March 14, 1920

[248] *Fort Worth Record-Telegram*, April 28, 1923

[249] Ibid.

[250] *Buffalo Courier*, June 10, 1923, *St. Louis Post Dispatch*, June 5, 1923, *San Francisco Chronicle*, July 22, 1923

[251] *Times Union*, January 2, 1927, The *Standard Union*, June 1, 1924

[252] The *Indiana Weekly Messenger*, June 4, 1925

[253] *Fort Collins Coloradoan*, July 24, 1925

[254] *El Paso Evening Post*, October 2, 1929, *El Paso Evening Post*, October 4, 1929

[255] Ibid.

[256] *Fort Worth Record-Telegram*, February 27, 1930

[257] *El Paso Herald Post*, October 13, 1933, The *Waco News*, October 14, 1934

[258] *Fort Worth Star-Telegram*, February 26, 1936

[259] www.ancestry.com Ruth Roach Salmon

[260] Ibid.

Relay Racing

[261] The *Kansas City Times*, April 28, 1925

[262] Ibid.

[263] The *Boston Globe*, May 2, 1907, https://accessgenealogy.com/connecticut/descantns-david-e-harding-mansfield.ma-htm

[264] The *Evening Herald*, April 3, 1908

[265] The *Boston Globe*, February 2, 1909

[266] https://ancestors.familysearch.org/en/LV7K-CJF/sumner-barton-kirby-1900-1976

[267] The *North Adams Transit*, September 1, 1923

[268] The *Sedalia Democrat*, April 26, 1925

[269] Ibid.

[270] Ibid.

[271] The *Boston Globe*, June 1, 1925

[272] Ibid.

[273] Ibid.

[274] The *Frankfort Index*, July 29, 1926

[275] The *Waco News Tribune*, November 3, 1926, The *Waco News Tribune*, October 28, 1926

[276] Ibid.

[277] Ibid.

[278] The *Brooklyn Daily Eagle*, November 13, 1927, The *Waco News Tribune*, November 8, 1926

[279] The *Brooklyn Daily Eagle*, November 13, 1927
[280] Ibid.
[281] Ibid.
[282] Ibid.
[283] Ibid.
[284] Ibid.
[285] *Auro News*, August 5, 1926, *Independent Courier*, September 10, 1926
[286] *Fort Worth Record-Telegram*, August 23, 1927
[287] The *Courier News*, October 19, 1927
[288] The *Messenger Inquirer*, October 20, 1927
[289] Ibid.
[290] The *Boston Globe*, November 4, 1928
[291] The *Miami Herald*, April 24, 1926
[292] *Fort Worth Star-Telegram*, May 31, 1929, The *Waco News Tribune*, May 10, 1950
[293] The *Waco News Tribune*, May 10, 1950
[294] Ibid.
[295] *Times Union*, October 21, 1936
[296] Ibid., *Fort Worth Star-Telegram*, March 20, 1936
[297] *Fort Worth Star-Telegram*, March 20, 1936
[298] *Fort Worth Star-Telegram*, September 5, 1941, *Fort Worth Star-Telegram*, June 23, 1942
[299] *Fort Worth Star-Telegram*, February 26, 1947
[300] *Fort Worth Star-Telegram*, May 9, 1950
[301] *Fort Worth Star-Telegram*, August 21, 1956
[302] *Tampa Bay Times*, May 26, 1959
[303] *Cowgirls of the Rodeo*, pg. 140-141

Horse Diving

[304] *The Last of the Wild West Cowgirls: A True Story*, pg. 22-24
[305] *Great Falls Tribune*, June 15, 1969
[306] The *Courier News*, July 20, 1903
[307] The *Courier News*, August 17, 1904
[308] The *Courier News*, November 15, 1904
[309] Ibid.
[310] Ibid.
[311] *Buffalo Courier*, April 25, 1905
[312] The *Courier News*, October 26, 1905
[313] The *Minneapolis Journal*, October 27, 1905
[314] The *Courier News*, October 2, 1905
[315] The *Courier News*, September 5, 1902, The *Courier News*, February 8, 1906
[316] The *Courier News*, February 8, 1906
[317] The *Courier News*, April 4, 1908
[318] The *Courier News*, March 18, 1908
[319] The *Courier News*, November 21, 1908
[320] The *Central New Jersey Home News*, December 4, 1908
[321] Ibid.

322 www.ancestry.com James Letcher Parker
323 *Detroit Free Press*, April 30, 1911
324 The *New York Times*, April 29, 1912
325 *Press Sun Bulletin*, January 8, 1912
326 The *Courier News*, July 10, 1913
327 The *Central New Jersey Home News*, June 26, 1913
328 The *Boston Globe*, March 8, 1915, *San Francisco Examiner*, June 24, 1915
329 *Los Angeles Record*, July 13, 1916
330 Ibid.
331 Ibid.
332 Ibid.
333 Ibid.
334 The *Salt Lake Herald Republican*, June 25, 1917
335 *Los Angeles Evening Express*, April 9, 1923
336 The *Courier News*, May 23, 1928, The *Courier News*, April 10, 1928
337 The *Courier News*, September 9, 1931, The *Courier News*, November 13, 1936
338 *Great Falls Tribune*, April 25, 1965
339 The *Courier News*, November 13, 1936
340 *The Akron Beacon Journal*, January 22, 1966

Trick Roping

341 Buffalo Bill Wild West Collection at the Center of the West MS 006 William F. Cody Collection
342 Parry Sister Collection Suffolk County Historical Society Library Archives
343 Ibid.
344 The *Decatur Herald*, August 24, 1913
345 The *Brooklyn Daily Eagle*, December 13, 1910
346 The *Butte Miner*, May 10, 1912
347 The *Seattle Star*, May 21, 1912, The *Victoria Daily Times*, May 25, 1912
348 The *Des Moines Tribune*, July 27, 1912, *Sioux City Journal*, July 24, 1912
349 *Boston Post*, June 17, 1913
350 The *Decatur Herald*, August 24, 1913
351 The *Buffalo Commercial*, August 1, 1914
352 Parry Sister Collection Suffolk County Historical Society Library Archives
353 Ibid.
354 *Capper's Weekly*, September 22, 1917
355 *Casper Daily Tribune*, March 1, 1921
356 *Casper Daily Tribune*, April 23, 1933
357 *Afton Star Valley Independent*, September 21, 1933 ✦

BIBLIOGRAPHY

Bryden, Wendy *The First Stampede Flores Ladue: The True Love Story of Florence and Guy Weadick and the Beginning of the Calgary Stampede* Touchstone Books New York, New York 2012

Day, Beth *America's First Cowgirl* Julian Messner, Inc New York, New York 1957

Gilchriest, Gail *The Cowgirl Companion: Big Skies, Buckaroos, Honky Tonks, Lonesome Blues, and Other Glories of the True West* Hyperion New York, New York 1993

Hanshew, Tracey *Oklahoma Rodeo Women* The History Press Mount Pleasant, South Carolina 2020

LeCompte, Mary *Cowgirls of the Rodeo: Pioneer Professional Athletes* University of Illinois Press Champagne, Illinois 1999

McGinnis, Vera *Rodeo Road: My Life As a Pioneer Cowgirl* Hastings House Publishing New York, New York 1974

Savage, Candace *Born to be a Cowgirl: A Spiritual Ride Through the Old West* Tricycle Press Berkeley, California 2001

Shirley, Glenn *Pawnee Bill: A Biography of Major Gordon W. Lillie* University of Nebraska Press Lincoln, Nebraska 1958

Stansbury, Kathryn *Lucille Mulhall: Wild West Cowgirl* Homestead Heirlooms Publishing Pewaukee, Wisconsin 1992

Turnbaugh, Kay *The Last of the Wild West Cowgirls: A True Story* Perigo Press Ventura County, California 2009

Wood-Clark, Sarah *Beautiful Daring Western Girls: Women of the Wild West Shows* Buffalo Bill Historical Center Cody, Wyoming 1991

Historical Manuscripts & Periodicals

Billboard Magazine February 21, 1914

Billboard Magazine September 2, 1916

Billboard Magazine April 4, 1912

Billboard Magazine March 22, 1913

Billboard Magazine June 4, 1927

Billboard Magazine March 23, 1929

Buffalo Bill Wild West Collection at the Center of the West MS 261 Lulu Bell

Buffalo Bill Wild West Collection at the Center of the West MS 006 William F. Cody Collection

Frontier Times Vol. 45, No. 6 October-November 1971 "Cowgirls—Rodeo's Sugar and Spice" by Milt Hinkle

Estelle Gilbert Papers, 1923-2003 Collection #: 064 Accession #: 1993.009, 2004.104 Mike Hastings Scrapbook National Cowboy Museum

Parry Sister Collection Suffolk County Historical Society Library Archives

Newspapers

Afton Star Valley Independent Afton, Wyoming September 21, 1933

The Akron Beacon Journal Akron, Ohio January 22, 1966

Albany Daily Democrat Albany, New York August 29, 1917

The Allentown Leader Allentown, Pennsylvania July 8, 1914

Amarillo Globe Times Amarillo, Texas June 24, 1929

The Ardmore Daily Press Ardmore, Oklahoma July 26, 1925

Argus-Leader Sioux Falls, South Dakota January 18, 1955

Arizona Daily Times Tucson, Arizona February 21, 1925

The Arizona Republic Phoenix, Arizona February 17, 1912

The Arizona Republic Phoenix, Arizona August 1, 1948

The Arizona Republic Phoenix, Arizona August 15, 1948

Asbury Park Press Asbury Park, New Jersey December 3, 1908

Ashland Weekly News Ashland, Wisconsin August 7, 1889

Bangor Daily News Bangor, Maine July 6, 1926

Barber County Index Medicine Lodge, Kansas August 30, 1923

Battle Creek Enquirer Battle Creek, Michigan July 12, 1930

The Beaver Press Beaver, Utah August 9, 1929

The Beemer Times Beemer, Nebraska June 14, 1923

Bennington Banner Bennington, Vermont September 10, 1920

Big Country Journal Abilene, Texas September 8, 2019

The Bobscobel Dial Bobscobel, Wisconsin March 9, 2000

The Boston Globe Boston, Massachusetts May 2, 1907

The Boston Globe Boston, Massachusetts February 2, 1909

The Boston Globe Boston, Massachusetts March 8, 1915

The Boston Globe Boston, Massachusetts September 28, 1921

The Boston Globe Boston, Massachusetts June 1, 1925

The Boston Globe Boston, Massachusetts November 4, 1928

The Boston Journal Boston, Massachusetts December 10, 1887

Boston Post Boston, Massachusetts June 17, 1913

Boston Post Boston, Massachusetts August 9, 1917

Bristow Daily Record Bristow, Oklahoma May 8, 1924

The Brooklyn Citizen Brooklyn, New York May 21, 1910

The Brooklyn Daily Eagle Brooklyn, New York December 13, 1910

The Brooklyn Daily Eagle Brooklyn, New York November 13, 1927

Brooklyn Times Union Brooklyn, New York April 24, 1914

Brooklyn Times Union Brooklyn, New York September 12, 1917

The Buffalo Commercial Buffalo, New York August 1, 1914

Buffalo Courier Buffalo, New York April 25, 1905

Buffalo Courier Buffalo, New York June 10, 1923

The Burwell Tribune Burwell, Nebraska August 8, 1925

The Butte Miner Butte, Montana April 19, 1903

The Butte Miner Butte, Montana May 10, 1912

The Butte Miner Butte, Montana July 4, 1916

Calgary Herald Calgary, Alberta, Canada September 6, 1912

Calgary Herald Calgary, Alberta, Canada July 13, 1917

Calgary Herald Calgary, Alberta, Canada August 28, 1919

Calgary Herald Calgary, Alberta, Canada September 2, 1919

Calgary Herald Calgary, Alberta, Canada July 3, 1970

Calgary Herald Calgary, Alberta, Canada July 8, 1994

The Californian Salinas, California July 9, 1962
The Caney Daily Chronicle Caney, Kansas October 22, 1920
Capper's Weekly Topeka, Kansas September 22, 1917
Casper Star Tribune Casper, Wyoming July 29, 1922
Casper Star Tribune Casper, Wyoming August 25, 1929
Casper Star Tribune Casper, Wyoming March 1, 1933
Casper Star Tribune Casper, Wyoming March 3, 1933
Casper Star Tribune Casper, Wyoming March 9, 1933
Casper Star Tribune Casper, Wyoming April 23, 1933
Casper Star Tribune Casper, Wyoming October 18, 1937
Casper Star Tribune Casper, Wyoming July 26, 1939
Casper Star Tribune Casper, Wyoming October 22, 1939
The Central New Jersey Home News New Brunswick, New Jersey December 4, 1908
The Central New Jersey Home News New Brunswick, New Jersey June 26, 1913
The Central New Jersey Home News New Brunswick, New Jersey April 3, 1936
Cheyenne State Leader Cheyenne, Wyoming March 5, 1919
The Chicago Live Stock World Chicago, Illinois May 19, 1910
The Chickasha Star Chickasha, Oklahoma February 13, 1920
Claflin Clarion Claflin, Kansas January 29, 1903
Clarion-Ledger Jackson, Mississippi October 7, 1939
The Clarksdale Press Register Clarksdale, Mississippi October 25, 1928
The Cleveland Enterprise Cleveland, Oklahoma September 22, 1905
The Collinsville News Collinsville, Oklahoma March 6, 1941
The Courier Waterloo, Iowa August 11, 1911
The Courier News Bridgewater, New Jersey September 5, 1902
The Courier News Bridgewater, New Jersey July 20, 1903
The Courier News Bridgewater, New Jersey August 17, 1904
The Courier News Bridgewater, New Jersey November 15, 1904
The Courier News Bridgewater, New Jersey April 25, 1905
The Courier News Bridgewater, New Jersey October 2, 1905
The Courier News Bridgewater, New Jersey October 26, 1905
The Courier News Bridgewater, New Jersey February 8, 1906
The Courier News Bridgewater, New Jersey March 18, 1908
The Courier News Bridgewater, New Jersey April 14, 1908
The Courier News Bridgewater, New Jersey November 21, 1908
The Courier News Bridgewater, New Jersey July 10, 1913
The Courier News Bridgewater, New Jersey October 19, 1927
The Courier News Bridgewater, New Jersey April 10, 1928
The Courier News Bridgewater, New Jersey May 23, 1928
The Courier News Bridgewater, New Jersey September 9, 1931
The Courier News Bridgewater, New Jersey September 22, 1934
The Courier News Bridgewater, New Jersey November 13, 1936
The Courier News Bridgewater, New Jersey September 14, 1953
Courier-Post Camden, New Jersey August 23, 1930
Coweta Times Star Coweta, Oklahoma June 30, 1926

Crook County Monitor Sundance, Wyoming September 1, 1899
The Custer County Chief Broken Bow, Nebraska October 6, 1893
The Daily Deadwood Pioneer-Times Deadwood, South Dakota June 7, 1924
The Daily Deadwood Pioneer-Times Deadwood, South Dakota July 2, 1924
The Daily News New York, New York November 4, 1927
The Daily News New York, New York August 23, 1936
The Daily Oklahoman Oklahoma City, Oklahoma December 27, 1940
Daily Press Newport News, Virginia February 19, 1933
The Daily Sentinel Grand Junction, Colorado September 13, 1919
The Daily Sentinel Grand Junction, Colorado September 9, 1920
The Daily Sentinel Grand Junction, Colorado June 6, 1922
The Davidsonian Davidson, North Carolina October 9, 1924
Dayton Daily News Dayton, Ohio May 10, 2001
The Dayton Herald Dayton, Ohio April 30, 1928
The Decatur Herald Decatur, Illinois August 24, 1913
Delphos Daily Herald Delphos, Ohio September 25, 1895
The Deming Headlight Deming, New Mexico February 23, 1923
Democrat and Chronicle Greece, New York June 28, 1937
The Democrat Opinion Woodland, California August 10, 1917
Des Moines Tribune Des Moines, Iowa June 17, 1911
Des Moines Tribune Des Moines, Iowa July 27, 1912
Des Moines Tribune Des Moines, Iowa August 22, 1916
Des Moines Tribune Des Moines, Iowa July 25, 1935
Detroit Free Press Detroit, Michigan April 30, 1911
Detroit Free Press Detroit, Michigan April 2, 1922
Dodge City Journal Dodge City, Kansas September 19, 1929
Douglass Tribune Douglass, Tribune January 28, 1916
Dubuque Telegraph Herald Dubuque, Iowa May 13, 1926
East Oregonian Pendleton, Oregon September 12, 1913
East Oregonian Pendleton, Oregon September 13, 1913
El Dorado Republican Shingle Springs, California November 3, 1916
El Paso Evening News El Paso, Texas September 23, 1929
El Paso Evening News El Paso, Texas September 27, 1929
El Paso Evening Post El Paso, Texas October 2, 1929
El Paso Evening Post El Paso, Texas October 4, 1929
El Paso Herald El Paso, Texas December 20, 1902
El Paso Herald Post El Paso, Texas July 21, 1900
El Paso Herald Post El Paso, Texas October 13, 1933
El Paso Times El Paso, Texas March 6, 1912
El Paso Times El Paso, Texas March 11, 1917
The El Reno Daily Tribune El Reno, Oklahoma August 31, 1936
The Elmcreek Beacon Elmcreek, Nebraska August 21, 1936
Elmore County Republicans Mountain Home, Idaho September 7, 1912
Elwood Daily Press Elwood, Indiana September 23, 1895
The Evening Herald Fall River, Massachusetts April 3, 1908

The Evening Herald Fall River, Massachusetts September 9, 1912
The Evening Standard Uniontown, Pennsylvania April 28, 1927
The Evening Sun Hanover, Pennsylvania May 12, 1915
The Evening Telegraph Providence, Rhode Island September 1, 1886
The Evening Times Sayre, Pennsylvania August 16, 1924
The Evening Times Sayre, Pennsylvania August 23, 1924
The Evening Times-Republican Marshalltown, Iowa July 27, 1912
Fitchburg Sentinel Fitchburg, Massachusetts September 28, 1917
Florence Morning News Florence, South Carolina October 20, 1925
Fort Collins Coloradoan Fort Collins, Colorado July 24, 1925
Fort Worth Record-Telegram Fort Worth, Texas March 3, 1919
Fort Worth Record-Telegram Fort Worth, Texas March 27, 1922
Fort Worth Record-Telegram Fort Worth, Texas April 28, 1923
Fort Worth Record-Telegram Fort Worth, Texas March 10, 1926
Fort Worth Record-Telegram Fort Worth, Texas August 23, 1927
Fort Worth Record-Telegram Fort Worth, Texas February 27, 1930
Fort Worth Star-Telegram Fort Worth, Texas March 13, 1917
Fort Worth Star-Telegram Fort Worth, Texas March 13, 1919
Fort Worth Star-Telegram Fort Worth, Texas April 10, 1919
Fort Worth Star-Telegram Fort Worth, Texas March 14, 1920
Fort Worth Star-Telegram Fort Worth, Texas November 26, 1920
Fort Worth Star-Telegram Fort Worth, Texas March 12, 1922
Fort Worth Star-Telegram Fort Worth, Texas April 27, 1923
Fort Worth Star-Telegram Fort Worth, Texas April 16, 1924
Fort Worth Star-Telegram Fort Worth, Texas November 2, 1924
Fort Worth Star-Telegram Fort Worth, Texas February 5, 1925
Fort Worth Star-Telegram Fort Worth, Texas March 11, 1925
Fort Worth Star-Telegram Fort Worth, Texas May 31, 1929
Fort Worth Star-Telegram Fort Worth, Texas March 7, 1931
Fort Worth Star-Telegram Fort Worth, Texas February 26, 1936
Fort Worth Star-Telegram Fort Worth, Texas March 20, 1936
Fort Worth Star-Telegram Fort Worth, Texas December 5, 1938
Fort Worth Star-Telegram Fort Worth, Texas September 5, 1941
Fort Worth Star-Telegram Fort Worth, Texas June 23, 1942
Fort Worth Star-Telegram Fort Worth, Texas February 26, 1947
Fort Worth Star-Telegram Fort Worth, Texas May 9, 1950
Fort Worth Star-Telegram Fort Worth, Texas August 21, 1956
The Frankfort Index Frankfort, Kansas July 29, 1926
The Galveston Daily News Galveston, Texas March 24, 1924
The Galveston Daily News Galveston, Texas May 16, 1925
The Garden City Telegram Garden City, Kansas August 7, 1919
The Gazette Cedar Rapids, Iowa June 19, 1925
The Gazette and Daily York, Pennsylvania May 17, 1938
The Grand Island Daily Independent Grand Island, Nebraska October 7, 1908
Great Falls Tribune Great Falls, Montana July 2, 1916

Great Falls Tribune Great Falls, Montana October 5, 1916
Great Falls Tribune Great Falls, Montana October 15, 1916
Great Falls Tribune Great Falls, Montana December 24, 1956
Great Falls Tribune Great Falls, Montana April 25, 1965
Great Falls Tribune Great Falls, Montana June 15, 1969
Harrisburg Telegram Harrisburg, Pennsylvania July23, 1917
Hartford Courant Hartford, Connecticut August 23, 1925
Hartford Courant Hartford, Connecticut February 4, 1930
Hartford Courant Hartford, Connecticut October 19, 1930
Hartford Courant Hartford, Connecticut August 18, 1957
The Haworth Herald Haworth, Oklahoma May 9, 1919
The Hugo Husonian Hugo, Oklahoma June 5, 1913
The Hutchinson Gazette Hutchinson, Kansas August 5, 1919
The Hutchinson Gazette Hutchinson, Kansas August 9, 1919
The Hutchinson Gazette Hutchinson, Kansas May 31, 1920
Independent Courier Clarence, Missouri September 10, 1926
Independent Observer Conrad, Montana June 21, 1923
The Indiana Weekly Messenger Indiana, Pennsylvania June 4, 1925
The Indianapolis Star Indianapolis, Indiana May 22, 1919
Jackson Hole Courier Jackson Hole, Wyoming March 2, 1933
Jackson Hole Courier Jackson Hole, Wyoming April 6, 1933
The Joliet News Joliet, Illinois June 6, 1907
Joplin Globe Joplin, Missouri September 27, 1923
The Kansas City Star Kansas City, Missouri September 4, 1905
The Kansas City Star Kansas City, Missouri January 21, 1907
The Kansas City Star Kansas City, Missouri September 16, 1912
The Kansas City Times Kansas City, Missouri May 25, 1912
The Kansas City Times Kansas City, Missouri December 12, 1924
The Kansas City Times Kansas City, Missouri April 28, 1925
The La Crosse Tribune La Crosse, Wisconsin July 4, 1926
Lead Daily Call Lead, South Dakota August 9, 1912
Little Falls Herald Little Falls, Minnesota July12, 1901
The Livestock Inspector Woodward, California October 15, 1899
Los Angeles Evening Express Los Angeles, California March 25, 1912
Los Angeles Evening Express Los Angeles, California February 18, 1913
Los Angeles Evening Express Los Angeles, California April 9, 1923
Los Angeles Record Los Angeles, California July 13, 1916
The Los Angeles Times Los Angeles, California October 23, 1925
The Los Angeles Times Los Angeles, California May 2, 1928
The Los Angeles Times Los Angeles, California August 5, 1932
Lubbock Morning Avalanche Lubbock, Texas December 24, 1940
The Manchester Journal Manchester Center, Vermont September 2, 1920
Manitoba Free Press Winnipeg, Manitoba, Canada March 31, 1914
The Messenger Inquirer Owensboro, Kentucky October 20, 1927
The Miami Herald Miami, Florida April 24, 1926

The Minneapolis Journal Minneapolis, Minnesota October 27, 1905
The Missoulian Missoula, Montana July 6, 1918
Monterey Daily Cypress Monterey, California January 1, 1913
The Morning Post Camden, New Jersey April 22, 1905
Mountain Gazette Jefferson, Vermont December 10, 1960
The Muscatine Journal Muscatine, Iowa August 3, 1921
Muskogee Daily Phoenix Muskogee, Oklahoma November 24, 1914
Napa Journal Napa Valley, California April 19, 1936
Natrona County Tribune Casper, Wyoming October 14, 1897
Natrona County Tribune Casper, Wyoming September 7, 1910
The Neihart Herald Neihart, Montana February 12, 1903
New Orleans Republican New Orleans, Louisiana August 24, 1873
The New York Times New York, New York April 29, 1912
The News-Herald Franklin, Pennsylvania May 24, 1924
The News Leader Staunton, Virginia November 2, 1920
The News Review Roseburg, Oregon September 19, 1924
North Adams Transit North Adams, Massachusetts September 1, 1923
North Adams Transit North Adams, Massachusetts October 30, 1924
Norwich Bulletin Norwich, Connecticut May 26, 1917
Oakland Tribune Oakland, California January 15, 1928
Ogden Standard Ogden, Utah February 27, 1915
The Oklahoma News Oklahoma City, Oklahoma August 18, 1935
The Oregon Daily Journal Portland, Oregon October 8, 1912
The Ottawa Herald Ottawa, Kansas August 4, 1920
The Ottumwa Daily Review Ottumwa, Iowa August 16, 1913
Palladium Item Richmond, Indiana May 30, 1919
The Pawnee Courier-Dispatch Pawnee, Oklahoma September 5, 1907
The Peabody Weekly Republican Peabody, Kansas September 16, 1887
The Philadelphia Inquirer Philadelphia, Pennsylvania June 7, 1908
The Philadelphia Inquirer Philadelphia, Pennsylvania July 4, 1926
The Pinedale Roundup Pinedale, Wyoming June 8, 1933
Pittsburgh Daily Post Pittsburgh, Pennsylvania July 16, 1916
The Pittsburgh Press Pittsburgh, Pennsylvania May 3, 1903
Pittston Gazette Pittston, Pennsylvania July 24, 1906
Press and Sun Bulletin Binghamton, New York January 8, 1912
The Pryor Creek Clipper Pryor, Oklahoma May 17, 1901
The Rock Island Argus Rock Island, Illinois September 22, 1936
St. Louis Dispatch St. Louis, Missouri January 8, 1907
The St. Louis Republic St. Louis, Missouri May 17, 1901
St. Louis Post Dispatch St. Louis, Missouri June 5, 1923
The Sacramento Bee Sacramento, California September 20, 1912
The Salt Lake Herald Republican Salt Lake City, Utah November 30, 1908
The Salt Lake Herald Republican Salt Lake City, Utah July 5, 1913
The Salt Lake Herald Republican Salt Lake City, Utah June 25, 1917
The Salt Lake Tribune Salt Lake, Utah October 16, 1915

San Francisco Chronicle San Francisco, California July 22, 1923
San Francisco Examiner San Francisco, California June 24, 1915
Scranton Tribune Scranton, Pennsylvania September 29, 1946
The Seattle Star Seattle, Washington May 21, 1912
The Sedalia Democrat Sedalia, Missouri April 26, 1925
Sioux City Journal Sioux City, Iowa July 24, 1912
Sioux City Journal Sioux City, Iowa June 22, 1913
The Skiatook News Skiatook, Oklahoma April 28, 1915
Spokane Chronicle Spokane, Washington August 30, 1919
Spokane Chronicle Spokane, Washington September 8, 1922
The Spokesman-Review Spokane, Washington May 21, 1912
The Spokesman-Review Spokane, Washington September 20, 1912
The Spokesman-Review Spokane, Washington August 2, 1913
The Spokesman-Review Spokane, Washington September 18, 1914
The Spokesman-Review Spokane, Washington September 20, 1914
The Spokesman-Review Spokane, Washington September 6, 1918
The Spokesman-Review Spokane, Washington September 5, 1922
The Spokesman-Review Spokane, Washington March 21, 1924
The Spokesman-Review Spokane, Washington March 25, 1924
The Spokesman-Review Spokane, Washington January 19, 1955
Springfield News-Sun Springfield, Ohio September 17, 2001
The Standard Union Brooklyn, New York June 24, 1906
The Standard Union Brooklyn, New York July 12, 1908
The Standard Union Brooklyn, New York August 1, 1916
The Standard Union Brooklyn, New York August 8, 1916
The Standard Union Brooklyn, New York June 1, 1924
Star Tribune Minneapolis, Minnesota May 29, 1922
The Tacoma Times Tacoma, Washington July 3, 1913
Tampa Bay Times Tampa, Florida May 26, 1959
The Tampa Times Tampa, Florida December 2, 1927
The Tiller and Toiler Larned, Kansas September 30, 1920
The Times Shreveport, Louisiana June 10, 1885
The Times Shreveport, Louisiana September 10, 1916
The Times Democrat Davenport, Iowa November 11, 1914
The Times-Tribune Scranton, Pennsylvania May 31, 1911
The Times-Tribune Scranton, Pennsylvania September 28, 1912
Times Union Albany, New York January 2, 1927
Times Union Albany, New York May 14, 1932
Times Union Albany, New York October 21, 1936
The Topeka Daily Capital Topeka, Kansas September 12, 1912
Tribune Stockman Farmer Cheyenne, Wyoming August 20, 1912
Tucson Citizen Tucson, Arizona January 29, 1936
Valley Morning Star Harlingen, Texas October 24, 2010
Vernon County News Viroqua, Wisconsin July 23, 1913
The Vernon Record Vernon, Texas February 10, 1925

The Victoria Daily Times Victoria, British Columbia, Canada May 25, 1912
The Waco News Tribune Waco, Texas October 28, 1926
The Waco News Tribune Waco, Texas November 3, 1926
The Waco News Tribune Waco, Texas November 4, 1926
The Waco News Tribune Waco, Texas October 15, 1929
The Waco News Tribune Waco, Texas October 14, 1934
The Waco News Tribune Waco, Texas May 10, 1950
Weekly Journal Miner Prescott, Arizona May 26, 1915
The Weekly Kansas City Star Kansas City, Missouri September 23, 1936
The Winnipeg Tribune Winnipeg, Manitoba, Canada August 12, 1913
The Winnipeg Tribune Winnipeg, Manitoba, Canada August 14, 1913
The Winnipeg Tribune Winnipeg, Manitoba, Canada August 15, 1913
The Winnipeg Tribune Winnipeg, Manitoba, Canada July 1, 1936
Woodland Daily Democrat Woodland, California June 20, 1930

Websites

www.abioh.byui.edu/specialcollections/westernstates/westernstatesrecorddetails.cfm
https://accessgenealogy.com/connecticut/descantns-david-e-harding-mansfield.ma-htm
https://ancestors.familysearch.org/en/LV7K-CJF/sumner-barton-Kirby-1900-1976
https://accessgenealogy.com/connecticut/descendants-david-e-harding-mansfield-ma-htm
   Descendants of David E. Harding of Mansfield, MA.
www.ancestry.com Pearl Biron
www.ancestry.com Rosa Belle "Prairie Rose Henderson" Gale
www.ancestry.com Hazel Hickey
www.ancestry.com May Manning
www.ancestry.com Alice Sommer
www.ancestry.com James Letcher Parker
www.ancestry.com Lulu Bell Parr
www.ancestry.com William James Parr
www.ancestry.com Jefferson Bryan Roach
www.ancestry.com Ruth Roach Salmon
www.ancestry.com Charlie C. Wilson
https://www.ancestry.com/search/collections/61048/ 1896-1943
https://www.aaalivestock.com/xtra/cowboy-heroes-50/ Tommy Kirnan—A Man of Many
   Talents by Jim Olson
https://www.buckit-list.com/inspiring-stories/profile-of-alice-sisty.html
https://faculty.chass.ncsu.edu/slatte/cowboy/essays/rodeo.htm Let's Rodeo by Richard
   W. Slatta
https://www.history.pcusa.org/services/records-management/records-congregations
   U.S. Presbyterian Church Records 1896-1943
http://sites.rootsweb.com/ksbarber/massey-joe-modainroundup.html
https://sites.rootsweb.com/~ksbarber/hastings_fox.html
https://townspirit.wordpress.com/2011/08/13/world-champion-saddle-bronc-rider
https://wesclark.com/burbank/bonnie_gray.html ❦

INDEX

Page numbers in **bold** indicate illustrations.

ABOUT THE AUTHOR

Chris Enss is a *New York Times* best-selling author who has been writing about women of the Old West for more than twenty years. She has penned more than forty published books on the subject. Her work has been honored with five Will Rogers Medallion Awards, two Elmer Kelton Book Awards, an Oklahoma Center for the Book Award, and was a Western Writers of America Spur Finalist. Her book *The Pinks: The First Women Detectives, Operatives, and Spies with the Pinkerton National Detective Agency* has been optioned by a major production company and is currently in development to become a television series. Enss' most recent works are *According to Kate: The Legendary Life of Big Nose Kate Elder, Love of Doc Holliday, No Place for a Woman: The Struggle for Suffrage in the Old West,* and *Iron Women: The Ladies Who Helped Build the Railroad.* ✦